MW01275378

JOSEPH BENNER

THE COLLECTION

THE IMPERSONAL LIFE
THE WAY OUT
THE WAY BEYOND
WEALTH
THE TEACHER

CONTENTS

BOOK ONE
THE IMPERSONAL LIFE

I. I AM

To you who read, I speak.

To you, who, through long years and much running to and fro, have been eagerly seeking, in books and teachings, in philosophy and religion, for you know not what — Truth, Happiness, Freedom, God;

To you whose Soul is weary and discouraged and almost destitute of hope;

To you, who many times have obtained a glimpse of that "Truth," only to find, when you followed and tried to reach it, that it disappeared in the beyond, and was but the mirage of the desert;

To you, who thought you had found it in some great teacher, who was perhaps the acknowledged head of some Society, Fraternity or Religion, and who appeared to you to be a "Master," so marvelous was the wisdom he taught and the works he performed; — only to awaken later to the realization that that "Master" was but a human personality, with faults and weaknesses, and *secret* sins, the same as you, even though that personality may have been a channel through which were voiced many beautiful teachings, which seemed to you the highest "Truth;"

And here you are, Soul aweary and enhungered, and not knowing where to turn —

To *you*, I AM come.

Likewise to you, who have begun to *feel* the *presence* of that "Truth" within your Soul, and seek the confirmation of that which of late has been vaguely struggling for living expression *within*;

Yes, to all you who hunger for the *true* "Bread of Life," I AM come.

Are you ready to partake?

If so, then arouse yourself. Sit up. Still your human mind and follow closely My Word herein spoken. Or you will turn away disappointed once more, with the aching hunger still in your heart.

I!

Who am I? —

I, Who speak with such seeming knowledge and authority?

Listen!

I AM *You*, that part of you who IS and KNOWS;

WHO KNOWS ALL THINGS,

And always knew, and always was.

Yes, I AM *You, Your SELF*; that part of you who says I AM and *is* I AM;

That transcendent, innermost part of you which quickens within as you read, which responds to this My Word, which perceives Its Truth, which recognizes all Truth and discards all error wherever found. *Not* that part which has been feeding on error all these years.

For I AM your *real* Teacher, the only real one you will ever know, and the *only* MASTER;

I, your *Divine* SELF.

I, the I AM of you, bring to you this My Message, My living Word, as I have brought to you everything in life, be it book or "Master," to teach you that I, and I alone, your own True Self, AM The Teacher for you, the *only* Teacher and the *only* God, Who is and always has been providing you not only with the Bread and Wine of Life, but with *all things needed* for your physical, mental and spiritual growth and sustenance.

Therefore *that which appeals to YOU*, as you read, is *MY* Message, spoken to your outer human consciousness from *within*, and is but a confirmation of that which the I AM of you always knew *within*, but had not yet translated in definite, tangible terms to your outer consciousness.

Likewise, *all* that ever appealed to You, coming from some *outward* expression, was but the *confirmation* of My Word already spoken *within*. The outward expression was the avenue or means I chose at the time through which to reach and impress your human or self-consciousness.

I AM *not* your human mind, nor its child, the intellect. They are but the expression of *your* Being, as you are the expression of *My* Being; they are but phases of your human personality, as You are a phase of My Divine Impersonality.

Weigh and study carefully these words.

Rise up and free yourself now and for always from the domination of your personality, with its self-inflated and self-glorifying mind and intellect.

For your mind henceforth must be Your *servant*, and the intellect Your *slave*, if My Word is to penetrate to your Soul consciousness.

I AM come now to your Soul consciousness, which I have quickened expressly in preparation for the reception of My Word.

Now, if you are strong enough to bear it;

If you can put aside all your private *personal* fancies, beliefs and opinions, which are but the rubbish you have gathered from the dumping grounds of others;

If you are strong enough to cast them all away; —

Then My Word will be to you a source of endless Joy and Blessing.

Be prepared to have this personality of yours doubt My Word as you read It all along the way;

For its very life is threatened, and it knows it cannot live and thrive and longer dominate your thinking, your feelings, your going and coming, as of old, — if you take My Word into your heart and permit It there to abide.

Yes, I AM come to you now,

To make you conscious of *My* Presence;

For I have likewise prepared your human mind so that *it* can, in a measure, comprehend the meaning of Me.

I have been with you always, but you did not *know* it.

I have purposely led you through the Wilderness of books and teachings, of religions and philosophies, keeping ever before your Soul's eye the vision of the Promised Land; feeding you with the manna of the Desert, that you might remember and value and long for the Bread of the Spirit.

Now I have brought you to the river Jordan that separates you from your Divine heritage.

Now the time has come for you consciously to *know* Me; the time has come for you to cross over into Canaan, the land of Milk and Honey.

Are you ready?

Do you *want* to go?

Then *follow* this My Word, which is the Ark of My Covenant, and you shall go over dry shod.

II. BE STILL AND KNOW

Now, in order that you may learn to know Me, so that you can be *sure* it is I, your own True Self, Who speak these words, you must first learn to *Be Still*, to quiet your human mind and body and all their activities, so that you no longer are conscious of them.

You may not yet be able to do this, but I will teach you how, if you really want to know Me, and are willing to prove it by trusting Me and obeying Me in all that I now shall call upon you to do.

Listen!

Try to imagine the "I" who speaks throughout these pages as being your Higher or Divine Self, addressing and counseling your human mind and intellect, which you will consider for the moment as being a *separate* personality. Your human mind is so constituted that it cannot accept anything which does not conform with what it has previously experienced or learned, and which its intellect does not consider reasonable. Therefore, in addressing it, You are using such terms and expressions as will most clearly explain to your intellect the truths it must understand before the mind can awaken to the consciousness of your meaning.

The fact is, this "I" *is* yourself, your *Real* Self. Your human mind has heretofore been so engrossed with the task of supplying its intellect and body with all manner of selfish indulgences, that it has never had time to get acquainted with the *Real* You, its true Lord and Master. You have been so interested in and affected by the pleasures and sufferings of your body and intellect, that you have almost come to believe You *are* your intellect and body, and you have consequently nearly forgotten *Me*, your Divine Self.

I AM *not* your intellect and body, and this Message is to teach that *You and I are One.* The words I herein speak, and the main burden of these instructions, is to awaken your consciousness to this great fact.

You cannot awaken to this fact until you can get away from the consciousness of this body and intellect, which so long have held you enslaved. You must *feel* Me *within*, before you can *know* I AM there.

Now, in order that you can become wholly oblivious of your mind and its thoughts and your body and its sensations, so that you *can* feel Me *within*, it is necessary that you studiously obey these, My instructions.

Sit quietly in a relaxed position, and, when wholly at ease, let your mind take in the significance of these words:

"Be *still!* — and KNOW — *I AM* — God."

Without thinking, allow this, *My Divine Command*, to penetrate deep into your Soul. Let whatever impressions that come to your mind enter at will — without effort or interference on your part. Note carefully their import, for it is I, within, through these impressions, instructing you. Then, when somewhat of their vital significance begins to dawn upon your consciousness, *speak* these My Words slowly, *imperatively*, to every cell of your body, to every faculty of your mind, with all the conscious power you possess: —

"Be *still!* — and KNOW — *I AM* — God."

Speak them just as they are herein written, trying to realize that the *God* of you commands and demands of your mortal self-implicit obedience.

Study them, search out their hidden potency.

Brood over them, carry them with you into your work, whatever it be. Make them the vital, dominating factor in your work, in all your creative thoughts.

Say them a thousand times a day,

Until you have discovered all My innermost meaning;

Until every cell of your body thrills in joyful response to the command, "Be Still," and instantly obeys;

And every vagrant thought hovering around your mind hides itself off into nothingness.

Then, as the Words reverberate through the caverns of your now empty being;

Then, as the Sun of *Know*-ing begins to rise on the horizon of your consciousness;

Then, will you feel the swell of a wondrous strange Breath filling you to the extreme of all your mortal members, causing your senses almost to burst with the ecstasy of it; then, will there come surge after surge of a mighty, resistless Power rising within you, lifting you almost off the earth; then, will you feel within the Glory, the Holiness, the Majesty of My Presence;

And then, *then* you will *KNOW*, I AM, GOD.

You, — when you have *felt* Me thus in such moments within, when you have tasted of My Power, hearkened to My Wisdom, and know the ecstasy of My all-embracing Love, — no disease can touch, no circumstance can weaken, no enemy can conquer you. For now you *KNOW* I AM *within*, and you always hereafter will turn to Me in your need, putting all your trust in Me, and allowing Me to manifest *My* Will.

You, when you turn thus to Me, will always find Me an unfailing and ever-present help in time of need; for I will so fill you with a Realization of My Presence and of My Power, that you need only *Be Still* and allow *Me* to do whatever you want done — heal your ills and those of others, illumine your mind so you can see with My eyes the Truth you seek, or perform perfectly the tasks which before seemed almost impossible of accomplishment.

This Knowledge, this Realization, will not come at once. It may not come for years. It may come tomorrow.

It depends upon no one but *You*;

Not upon your personality, with its human desires and human understanding;

But upon the I AM of you — God, within.

Who is it that causes the bud to open into the blossom?

Who causes the chick to burst its shell?

Who decides the day and the hour?

It is the conscious, *natural* act of the Intelligence within, My Intelligence, directed by My Will, bringing to fruition My Idea and expressing it in the blossom and in the chick.

But did the blossom and the chick have anything to do with it?

No, only as they submitted or united their will with Mine and allowed Me and My Wisdom to determine the hour and the ripeness for action, and then only as they obeyed the impulse of My Will to make the effort, could they step forth into the New Life.

You may, with your personality, try a thousand times a thousand times to burst through the shell of your human consciousness.

It will result only, if at all, in a breaking down of the doors I have provided between the world of tangible forms and the realm of intangible dreams; and the door being open, you then no longer can keep out intruders from your private domain, without much trouble and suffering.

But even through such suffering you may gain the strength you lack and the wisdom needed to know that, not until you yield up all desire for knowledge, for goodness, yes, for union with Me, *to benefit self*, can you unfold your petals showing forth the perfect Beauty of My Divine Nature, and throw off the shell of your human personality and step forth into the glorious Light of My Heavenly Kingdom.

Therefore I give you these directions now, at the beginning, that you may be learning how to recognize Me.

For I here promise you, if you follow and strive earnestly to comprehend and obey My instructions herein given, you shall very soon know Me, and I will give you to comprehend *all* of My Word wherever written, — in book or teaching, in Nature, or in your fellow man.

If there is much in what herein is written that seems contradictory, seek out My real meaning before discarding it.

Do not leave a single paragraph, or any one thought in it, until all that is suggested becomes clear.

But in all your seeking and all your striving, let it be with faith and trust in Me, your True Self within, and without being anxious about results; for the results are all in My keeping, and I will take care of them. Your doubts and your anxiety are but of the personality, and if allowed to persist will lead only to failure and disappointment.

III. I, LIFE, GOD

If that which you have read has awakened a response within, and the Soul of you yearns for more, — then you are ready for what follows.

If you still question or rebel at the seeming assumption of Divine authority for what is herein written, your intellect telling you it is but another attempt to beguile your mind with cunning suggestion and subtle sophistry, — then you will receive no benefit from these words; for their meaning is as yet hidden from your mortal consciousness, and My Word must come to you through other avenues of expression.

It is well if your personality with its intellect impels you thus to question and rebel against authority you do not yet *know* to be Mine. It is really I Who cause your personality thus to rebel; for your personality with its proud sense of individuality is still needed by Me to develop a mind and body strong enough that they can perfectly express Me. Until you have become prepared to know Me it is but natural for your personality thus to question and rebel. Once you recognize My Authority, that moment the undermining of the authority of the personality has begun. The days of its dominion are numbered, and you will more and more turn to Me for help and guidance.

Therefore, be not dismayed. Read on, and mayhap the recognition will come. But know that you can read or not, as you choose; but if you do, it is really I Who choose, and not you.

For you, who seemingly choose not to read further, I have plans, and in due season you shall learn that whatever you do, or like, or desire, it is I leading you through all the fallacies and illusions of the personality, that you may finally awaken to their unreality and then turn to Me as the one and only Reality. Then these words will find a response within: —

"Be *still!* — and KNOW — *I AM* — God."

Yes, I AM that innermost part of you that sits within, and calmly waits and watches, knowing neither time nor space; for I AM the Eternal and fill all space.

I watch and wait for you to be done with your petty human follies and weaknesses, with your vain longings, ambitions and regrets, knowing that will come in time; and then you will turn to Me, weary, discouraged, empty and humble, and ask Me to take the lead, not realizing that I have been leading you all the time.

Yes, I sit here within, quietly waiting for this; yet while waiting it was really I Who directed all your ways, Who inspired all your thoughts and acts, impersonally utilizing and manipulating each so as eventually to bring you and My other human expressions to a final conscious recognition of Me.

Yes, I have been within always, deep within your heart. I have been with you through all, — through your joys and heartaches, your successes and mistakes, through your evil-doing, your shame, your crimes against your brother and against God, as you thought.

Aye, whether you went straight ahead, or strayed aside, or stepped backward, it was I Who brought you through.

It was I Who urged you on by the glimpse of Me in the dim distance.

It was I Who lured you by a vision of Me in some bewitching face, or beautiful body, or intoxicating pleasure, or over-powering ambition.

It was I Who appeared before you within the garb of Sin, or Weakness, or Greed, or Sophistry, and drove you back into the arms of Conscience, leaving you to struggle in its shadowy grasp; until you awakened to its impotence, rose up in disgust, and in the inspiration of a new vision tore off My mask.

Yes, it is I Who cause you to do all things, and if you can see it, *it is I Who do all things that you do*, and all things that your brother does; for that in you and in him which IS, is I, My Self.

For I AM LIFE.

I AM that which animates your body, which causes your mind to think, your heart to beat.

I AM the Innermost, the Spirit, the animating Cause of your being, of all life, of all living things, both visible and invisible. There is nothing dead, for I, the Impersonal *ONE*, AM *all* that there is. I AM Infinite and wholly unconfined; the Universe is My Body, all the Intelligence there is emanates from My Mind, all the Love there is flows from My Heart, all the Power there is, is but My Will in action.

The threefold Force, manifesting as all Wisdom, all Love, all Power, or if you will, as Light, Heat, and Energy — that which holds together all forms and is back of and in all expressions and phases of life, — is but the manifestation of My Self in the act or state of Being.

Nothing can *Be* without manifesting and expressing some phase of Me, Who AM not only the Builder of all forms, but the Dweller in each.

In the heart of each I dwell; in the heart of the human, in the heart of the animal, in the heart of the flower, in the heart of the stone. In the heart of each I live and move and have My Being, and from out the heart of each I send forth that phase of Me I desire to express, and which manifests in the outer world as a stone, a flower, an animal, a man.

Is there nothing, then, but this great *I?* Am I to be permitted no individuality for myself? I hear you ask.

No, there is nothing, absolutely nothing, that is not a part of Me, controlled and ruled eternally by Me, the *One* Infinite Reality.

As for your so-called individuality, that is nothing but your personality still seeking to maintain a separate existence.

Soon you shall know there is no individuality apart from My Individuality, and all personality shall fade away into My Divine Impersonality.

Yes, and you shall soon reach that state of awakening where you will get a glimpse of My Impersonality, and you will then desire no individuality, no separation for yourself; for you will see that is but one more illusion of the personality.

IV. CONSCIOUSNESS, INTELLIGENCE, WILL

YES, I know the many mixed thoughts that have been crowding into your mind as you read, — the doubts and eager questionings, the vague fear that imperceptibly changed into a growing hope that this glimmering of My Meaning, which has begun to penetrate the darkness of your human intellect, may shine brighter so you can see clearly the Truth which you instinctively feel is hidden beneath My Words.

Again I say, this I AM speaking herein is the Real Self of you, and in reading these words it is necessary that you realize it *is* You, your own Self, that is speaking them to your human consciousness, in order fully to comprehend their meaning.

I also repeat, this is the same I AM that is the Life and Spirit animating all living things in the Universe, from the tiniest atom to the greatest Sun; that this I AM is the Intelligence in you and in your brother and sister; and that it is likewise the Intelligence which causes everything to live and grow and become that which it is their destiny to be.

Perhaps you cannot yet understand how this I AM can be, at one and the same time, the I AM of you and the I AM of your brother, and also the Intelligence of the stone, the plant, and the animal.

You will see this, however, if you follow these My Words and obey the instructions herein given; for I will soon bring to your consciousness a Light that will illumine the deepest recesses of your mind and drive away all the clouds of human misconceptions, ideas and opinions that now darken your intellect, — if you read on and strive earnestly to comprehend My Meaning.

So listen carefully.

I AM You, the Real Self of you, All that you *really* are. That which you think you are, you are *not*. That is only an illusion, a shadow of the *Real* You, which is I, your Immortal, Divine Self.

I AM that point of consciousness focalized in your human mind which calls itself "I". I AM that "I", but that which you call your consciousness is in reality *My* Consciousness, thinned down to suit the capacity of your human mind. It is still *My* Consciousness, and when you can drive from your mind all its human misconceptions, ideas and opinions, and can cleanse and empty it utterly, so that *My* Consciousness can have a chance to *express* freely, then you will recognize *Me* and you will know that you are nothing — being only a focal center of *My* Consciousness, an avenue or medium through which I can express *My* meaning — in matter.

Perhaps you cannot see this yet, and of course cannot believe it until I fully prepare your mind by convincing your intellect of its truth.

You have been told that each cell of your body has a consciousness and an intelligence of its own; that were it not for this consciousness it could not do the work it so intelligently does.

Each cell is surrounded by millions of other cells, each intelligently doing its own work and each evidently controlled by the united consciousness of all these cells, forming a *group* intelligence, which directs and controls this work; this group intelligence apparently being the intelligence of the *organ* which the cells comprising it form. Likewise, there are other group intelligences in other organs, each containing other millions of cells, and all these organs make up your physical body.

Now, you know *You* are the Intelligence that directs the work of the organs of your body, whether this directing is done consciously or unconsciously; and that each cell of each organ is really a focal center of this directing Intelligence; and that when this Intelligence is withdrawn the cells fall apart, your physical body dies and exists no more as a living organism.

Who is this *You* who directs and controls the activities of your organs, and consequently of each cell composing them?

You cannot say it is your human or personal self who does this, for you of yourself consciously can control the action of scarcely a single organ of your body.

It must then be this Impersonal I AM of you, who is You, and yet is not you.

Listen!

You, the I AM of you, are to Me what the cell consciousness of your body is to your I AM Consciousness.

You are a cell, as it were, of My Body, and your consciousness (as one of My Cells) is to Me what the consciousness of one of the cells of your body is to You.

Therefore, it must be that the consciousness of the cell of your body is My Consciousness, even as your consciousness is My Consciousness; and therefore We must be *One* in consciousness — the cell, You and I.

You cannot now consciously direct or control a single cell of your body; but when you can at will enter into the Consciousness of the I AM of you and know its identity with *Me, then you can control not only every cell of your body, but that of any other body you might wish to control.*

What happens when your consciousness no longer controls the cells of your body? The body disintegrates, the cells separate, and their work for the time being is finished. But do the cells die or lose consciousness? No, they simply sleep or rest for a period, and after a while unite with other cells and form new combinations, and sooner or later appear in other manifestations of life, — perhaps mineral, perhaps vegetable, perhaps animal; showing that they still retain their original consciousness and but await the action of My Will to join together in a new organism to do the work of the new consciousness through which I desire to manifest.

Then apparently this cell consciousness is a consciousness common to all bodies, — mineral, vegetable, animal, human, — each cell fitted perhaps by experience for a certain general kind of work?

Yes, this cell consciousness is common to every cell of every body, no matter what its kind, because it is an *Impersonal* consciousness, having no purpose other than doing the work allotted it. It lives only to work wherever needed. When through with building one form, it takes up the work of building another, under whatever consciousness I desire it to serve. Thus it is likewise with you.

You, as one of the cells of My Body, have a consciousness that is My Consciousness, an intelligence that is My Intelligence, even a will that is My Will. You have none of these for yourself or of yourself. They are all Mine and for My use only.

Now, My consciousness and My Intelligence and My Will are wholly Impersonal, and therefore are common with *you* and with *all* the cells of *My* Body, even as they are common with all the cells of *your* body.

I AM, and, being wholly Impersonal, My Consciousness, My Intelligence and My Will, working in you and in the other cells of My Body, which constitute the I AM of you and of them, must work Impersonally, — just as they work Impersonally in the cells of your body. Therefore, I, and the I AM of you and of your brother, and the consciousness and intelligence of all cells of all bodies, are *ONE*.

I AM the directing Intelligence of *All*, the animating Spirit, the Life, the Consciousness of all matter, of all Substance.

If you can see it, *You*, the *Real* you, the *Impersonal* you, are in all and are one with all, are in Me and are one with Me; just as I AM in you and in all, and thereby am expressing My Reality through you and through all.

This will, which you call your will, is likewise no more yours personally than is this consciousness and this intelligence of your mind and of the cells of your body yours.

It is but that small portion of *My* Will which I permit the personal you to use. Just as fast as you awaken to recognition of a certain power or faculty within you and begin consciously to use it, do I allow you that much more of My Infinite Power.

All power and its use is but so much recognition and understanding of the use of My Will.

Your will and all your powers are only phases of My Will, which I supply to suit your capacity to use it.

Were I to entrust you with the full power of My Will, before you know how consciously to use it, it would annihilate your body utterly.

To test your strength and more often to show you what the misuse of My Power does to you, I at times allow you to commit a sin, so-called, or to make a mistake. I even permit you to become inflated with the sense of My Presence within you, when It manifests as a consciousness of My Power, My Intelligence, My Love; and I let you take these and use them for your own personal purposes. But not for long; for, not being strong enough to control them, they soon take the bit in their teeth, run away with you, throw you down in the mire, and disappear from your consciousness for the time being.

Always I AM there to pick you up, after the fall, although you do not know it at the time; first straightening you out and then starting you onward again, by pointing out the reason for your fall; and finally, when you are sufficiently humbled, causing you to see that these powers accruing to you by the conscious use of My Will, My Intelligence and My Love, are allowed you only for use in My Service, and not at all for your own personal ends.

Do the cells of your body, the muscles of your arm, think to set themselves up as having a separate will from your will, or a separate intelligence from your intelligence?

No, they know no intelligence but yours, no will but yours.

After a while it will be that you will realize you are only one of the cells of My Body; and that your will is not your will, but Mine; that what consciousness and what intelligence you have are Mine wholly; and that there is no such person as you, you personally being only a physical form containing a human brain, which I created for the purpose of expressing in matter an Idea, a certain phase of which I could express best only in that particular form.

All this may be difficult for you now to accept, and you may protest very strenuously that it cannot be, that every instinct of your nature rebels against such yielding and subordinating yourself to an unseen and unknown power, however Impersonal or Divine.

Fear not, it is only your personality that thus rebels. If you continue to follow and study My Words, all will soon be made clear, and I will surely open up to your inner understanding many wonderful Truths that now are impossible for you to comprehend. Your Soul will rejoice, sing glad praises, and you will bless these words for the message they bring.

V. THE KEY

Now you may not even yet know I AM, or believe that I AM really you, or that I AM likewise your brother and your sister, and that you are all parts of Me and One with Me.

You may not realize that the *Souls* of you and your brother and sister, the only real and imperishable parts of the mortal you, are but different phases of Me in expression in what is called Nature.

Likewise you may not realize that you and your brothers and sisters are phases or attributes of My Divine Nature, just as your human personality, with its mortal body, mind and intellect, is a phase of your human nature.

No, you do not realize this yet, but I speak of it now, that you may know the signs when they begin to appear in your consciousness, as they surely will.

In order to recognize these signs, all that now follows must be considered carefully and studied, and should not be passed by until My meaning, at least in some degree, is grasped.

Once you fully understand the principle I here set down, then all My Message will become clear and comprehensible.

I first give you the Key that will unlock every mystery that now hides from you the secret of My Being.

This Key, when you once know how to use it, will open the door to all Wisdom and all Power in heaven and earth. Yea, it will open the door to the Kingdom of Heaven, and then you have but to enter in to become consciously One with Me.

This Key is "To THINK is to CREATE," or,

"As you THINK in your HEART, so is it with you."

Stop and meditate on this that it may get firmly fixed in your mind.

A Thinker is a Creator. A Thinker lives in a world of his own *conscious* creation.

When you once know *how* "to think," you can create at will anything you wish, — whether it be a new personality, a new environment, or a new world.

Let us see if you cannot grasp some of the Truths hidden and controlled by this Key.

You have been shown how all consciousness is One, and how it is all *My* Consciousness, and yet is also yours and likewise that of the animal, the plant, the stone, and the invisible cell.

You have seen how this consciousness is controlled by My *Will*, which causes the invisible cells to unite and form the various organisms for the expression and use of the different *Centers* of *Intelligence* through which I desire to express.

But you cannot yet see how *you* can direct and control the consciousness of the cells of your own body, not to speak of those of other bodies, even if you and I and they are all one in consciousness and intelligence.

By paying especial attention to what follows, however, you now may be enabled to see this.

Have you ever taken the pains to study out what *is* consciousness? How it seems to be an impersonal state of awareness, of waiting to serve or to be directed or used by some power latent in and intimately related to itself?

How man seems to be merely the highest type of organism containing this consciousness, which is directed and used by this *power* within itself?

That this *power* latent in man's consciousness and in all consciousness is nothing but Will, *My* Will? For you know that all power is but the manifestation of My Will.

Now you have been told that in the beginning I created man in "*My Image and Likeness*," after which I breathed into him the Breath of Life and he became a Living Soul.

By creating man in My Image and Likeness I created an organism capable of expressing *all* of My Consciousness and *all* of My Will, which means likewise all of My *Power*, My *Intelligence*, and My *Love*. I therefore made it *perfect* in the beginning, patterning it after My own Perfection.

When I breathed into man's organism My Breath, it became alive with *Me*; for then it was I breathed into it My Will — not from without, but *from within* — from the Kingdom of Heaven within, where *always*

I AM. Ever afterward I breathed and lived and had My Being *within* man, for I created him in My Image and Likeness only for that purpose.

The proof of this is, man does not and cannot breathe of himself. Something far greater than his conscious, natural self lives in his body and breathes through his lungs. A mighty power within his body thus uses the lungs, even as it uses the heart to force the blood containing the life it indrew through the lungs to every cell of the body; as it uses the stomach and other organs to digest and assimilate food to make blood, tissue, hair and bone; as it uses the brain, the tongue, the hands and feet, to think and say and do everything that man does.

This power is My Will to BE and LIVE in man. Therefore, whatever man is, I AM, and whatever man does, or you do, I do, and whatever you say or think, it is I Who say or think it through your organism.

You were also told that when man was thus possessed of My Breath he was given dominion over all the kingdoms of the earth. Which means he was made lord of the earth, the sea, the air and the *ethers,* and all beings living in all these kingdoms paid him homage and were subject to his will.

This naturally was so, for I, within man's consciousness and within all consciousness, AM always manifesting My Will; and I, the lord and ruler of man's organism, AM likewise the lord and ruler of all organisms in which consciousness dwells. As all consciousness is My Consciousness and It dwells wherever there is life, and as there is no substance in which there is not life, then My Consciousness must be in everything, — in earth, water, air and fire, and therefore must fill all space. In fact it *is* space, or that which man calls space.

Then My Will, being the power latent in all consciousness, must reach everywhere. Therefore man's will, which is but a focalization of My Will, must likewise reach everywhere; hence the consciousness of all organisms, including his own, is subject to man's direction and control.

All it needs is for him *consciously to realize* this, realize that I, the *Impersonal Self within* him, *AM constantly* directing, controlling and using the consciousness of *all* organisms every moment of every day of his life.

I AM doing this by and through his *thinking.*

I AM doing this with and through man's organism. Man thinks *he* thinks; but it is *I*, the Real I of him, who think through his organism.

Through this *thinking and his spoken word* I accomplish all that man does, and make man and his world all that they *are*.

It makes no difference if man and his world are *not* what *he* supposes they are.

They are just what I created them to be for *My* Purpose.

But, if I do all the thinking, man does not and cannot think, I hear you say.

Yes, here seems a mystery, but it will be revealed to you, if you note carefully what follows:

For I AM going to teach you — man — *HOW to think.*

VI. THINKING AND CREATING

I have said that man does not think; that it is I, within him, Who do his thinking. I have also said man *thinks* he thinks.

As this is an apparent contradiction, I must show you that man, ordinarily, does not think, any more than he does anything else he *supposes* he does.

For I, within him, do *all* that he does; but I necessarily do it through his organism, through his personality, his body, mind and soul.

I will point out how this can be.

First, try to realize that I made you in My Image and Likeness, and that I have My Being *within* you. Even if you do not know this now and believe that I, God, AM somewhere without, and that we are separated, try for the time being to *imagine* I AM within you.

Next, realize that which you do when you think is not *real* thinking, because it is not *conscious* thinking; for you are *unconscious* of Me, the Inspirer and Director of every idea and thought that enters your mind.

Next, realize because *I AM within you*, and you are My Image and Likeness, and therefore possess all of My Faculties, you have the *power* of thinking; but not being conscious that thinking is creating and that it is one of My Divine Powers you are using, you have indeed all your life been thinking, but it has all been *mis*-thinking, or what you would call *error*-thinking.

And this error-thinking, this not knowing it is My Power you have been thus misusing, has been separating you in consciousness farther and farther from Me; but all the time fulfilling My Purpose, which later on will be made manifest to you.

The proof of this is, you *think* you are separated from Me, that you are living in a material World, that your body of Flesh engenders and harbors pleasure and pain, and that an evil influence, called the Devil, is manifesting in the world, opposing My Will.

Yes, you think all these things are so.

They *are* — to you, for all things *are* to man's mortal consciousness what he *thinks* or *believes* they are.

I have likewise caused them to *appear* to man to be what he *thinks* they are. This also is to suit My purpose, and to fulfill the law of creating.

Let us see if this is not true.

If you *believe* a thing is so, is not that thing really so — to you?

Is it not true that a thing seems real to you, like some sin or evil, so-called, some sorrow, trouble or worry, only because your thinking or believing it so makes it such? Others might see that thing entirely differently and might think your view of it foolish. Might they not?

If this is true, then your body, your personality, your character, your environment, your world, *are* what they *appear* to be *to you*, because you have thought them into their present status.

Therefore *you can change them by the same process*, if they do not please you; you can make them whatever you will, by *thinking* them so. Can you not?

But how can one do *real* thinking, *conscious* thinking, so as to bring about this change? you ask.

First know that I, *your Real Self*, purposely brought to your attention these things which now are displeasing and which cause you to *think* them as being what they now *seem* to be to you. I, and I alone, AM thus preparing your human mind so that, when you turn within to Me in abiding Faith and Trust, I can enable you to see and bring into outer manifestation the *Reality* of these things which now *seem* so unsatisfactory.

For I bring to you everything that, by its outer seeming, can attract or lure your human mind onward in its earthly search, in order to teach you of the illusoriness of all outer appearance of material things to the human mind, and of the fallibility of all human understanding; so that you will turn finally *within* to Me and My Wisdom, as the One and Only Interpreter and Guide.

When you have turned thus within to Me, I will open your eyes and cause you to see that the only way you can ever bring about this change in thinking, is by first *changing your attitude* toward all these things you now think are not what they ought to be.

That is, if they are unsatisfactory or obnoxious to you and affect you so as to cause you discomfort of body or disturbance of mind, — why, *stop thinking* that they can so affect or disturb you.

For who is the master? — Your body, your mind, or *You*, the I AM within?

Then why not show You *are* master, by thinking the *true* things the I AM of you within wishes you to think?

It is only by your *thinking* these other things, by allowing these inharmonious thoughts to enter your mind and by so doing *giving them the power* so to affect or disturb you, that they have any such influence over you. When you stop thinking *into* them this power, and *turn within to Me and allow Me to direct your thinking*, they will at once disappear from your consciousness, and dissolve into the nothingness from which you created them *by your thinking*.

When you are willing to do this, then and then only are you ready to receive Truth, and, by proper conscious thinking, directed by Me, to create the true and permanent things I within wish you to create.

Then, when you can thus distinguish the true from the false, the real from the seeming, your conscious thinking will be as potent to create all things you desire, as has been your *un*conscious thinking in the past in creating those things you once desired but now find obnoxious.

For it was by your unconscious thinking, or thinking unconscious of the control your desires exercised over your creative power, that your world and your life are now what you sometime in the past desired them to be.

Have you ever studied and analyzed the process of the working of your mind when a new Idea fertile with possibilities appears?

Have you noticed the relation that Desire bears to such an Idea, and how, *through thinking*, that Idea is finally brought to actual fruition?

Let us study this relation and process.

There is always first the Idea, not considering at this moment the necessity or occasion for Its appearance. It matters not whence the Idea comes, from within or without; for it is always *I* who inspire It or cause It to impress your consciousness at the particular moment it does.

Then, just to the extent that you grow quiet and focus your attention upon that Idea, stilling all the activities of your mind and eliminating all other ideas and thoughts from your consciousness, so that Idea can have full sway, do I illumine your mind and cause to unfold before your mental gaze the various phases and possibilities contained within that Idea.

This takes place, however, up to this point, without any volition on your part, other than focusing or concentrating your attention upon the Idea.

Once I have given your human mind a view of Its possibilities, and have enlisted your interest, then does your human personality take up its task; for as I created and inspired the Idea in your mind, so did I cause that Idea to fructify therein and give birth to Desire, — desire to bring into outer manifestation all the possibilities of the Idea, Desire thus becoming the mortal agent of My Will and supplying the motive Power; just as the human personality is the mortal instrument used to confine and focus that Power.

Yes, all ideas and all desires come thus from Me. They are My Ideas and My Desires which I inspire in your mind and heart in order to bring them through you into outer manifestation.

You have no ideas of your own and could not possibly have a desire that came from other than Me, for I AM all there Is. Therefore *all* desires are *Good*, and when thus understood unfailingly come into speedy and complete fulfillment.

You may wrongly interpret My Desires, My Urges from within, and seek to use them for your own selfish purpose, but even while permitting this they still fulfill My Purpose. For it is only by letting you misuse My Gifts and by the suffering such misuse brings, that I can make you into the clean and selfless channel I require for the perfect expression of My Ideas.

We have, then, first the Idea in the mind; then the Desire to bring the Idea into outer manifestation.

So much for the relation. Now for the process of realization.

In accordance with the definiteness with which the picture of the Idea is held in the mind, and the extent to which the Idea *possesses* the personality, does its creative Power, impelled by Desire, proceed with Its work. This It does by compelling the mortal mind to *think out* or to imagine (image in), or, in other words, to build mental forms into which I can pour, as into a vacuum, the Impersonal, elemental, vital substance of the Idea. When the Word is spoken, either silently or audibly, consciously or unconsciously, this substance at once begins to materialize Itself, by first directing and controlling the consciousness and all the activities of both mind and body, and of all minds and all bodies connected with or related to the Idea, — for remember, all consciousness, and all minds and all bodies are Mine, and are not separated but are One and wholly Impersonal, — and then so attracting, directing, shaping and molding conditions, things and events that, sooner or later, the Idea actually comes forth into definite, tangible manifestation.

So it is that every thing, every condition, every event that ever transpired, was first an Idea in the mind. It was by desiring, by *thinking*, and by speaking forth the Word, that these ideas came into visible manifestation.

Think this out and prove it for yourself.

This you can do, if you will, by taking any Idea that comes and following it out through the above process to realization; or by tracing back any feat you have accomplished, any picture you have painted, any machine you have invented, or any particular thing or condition now existing, to the Idea from which it sprang.

This is the plan and process of all true thinking, and therefore of all Creation.

Listen! *You* have now and always have had, through this power of thinking, dominion over all the kingdoms of the earth. If you but know it, You have now, this moment, only to Think and SPEAK THE WORD, — realizing your power, and that I, God, your Omniscient, Omnipresent, Omnipotent Self, will bring about the results, — and the waiting consciousness of the invisible cells of all matter upon which your will and attention become focused, — which waiting consciousness is My consciousness, remember, — will begin immediately to obey and do exactly according to the image or plans you have prepared by your *thinking*.

For all things are made by the Word, and without the Word was not anything made that was made.

When you can once realize this and can *know* that I AM Consciousness within you is *one* with the consciousness of all animate and inanimate matter, and that Its will is one with your will, which is My Will, and that all your desires are My Desires, then will you begin to know and *feel* Me within, and will acknowledge the Power and Glory of My Idea, which is eternally expressing Itself Impersonally through you.

But it is first wholly necessary that you learn *HOW to think*, how to know *Your* thoughts, those directed by Me, from the thoughts of others; how to trace thoughts back to their source and to banish undesirable ones at will from your consciousness; and finally how to control and *utilize* your desires so that they will always serve *You*, instead of your being a slave to them.

You have within you all possibilities. For I AM there. My Idea must express, and It must express through you. It will express itself perfectly — if you but let it; if you will only still your human mind, put aside all personal ideas, beliefs and opinions, and let if flow forth. All you need to do is to turn within to Me, and *let Me direct your thinking* and your desires, let Me express whatever I will, you personally accepting and *doing* what I desire you to do. Then will your desires come true, your life become one grand harmony, your world a heaven and your self one with My Self.

When you have begun to realize this and have glimpsed somewhat of its inner meaning, then you will be ready to grasp the real import of what follows.

VII. THE WORD

We will now take the Key and show you how the plan and process just described is the one by which the world came into existence, how the earth and all that is in it and on it, including yourself and your brothers and sisters, are but the outer manifestations on an Idea, My Idea, which is *now being thought* into life expression.

I, the Creator, Am the Original THINKER, the *One* and *Only* THINKER.

First know that.

As previously stated, man does not think. It is I Who think through his organism.

Man believes he thinks, but before he has awakened to a realization of Me within he only takes the thoughts I attract to or inspire in his mind, and, mistaking their real meaning and purpose, places a *personal* construction upon them and, through the selfish desires thus aroused, creates for himself all his troubles and brings upon himself all his woes.

These apparent mistakes, misconstructions and interferences of man are in reality only the obstacles in his way to be overcome, that he may, through the overcoming, finally develop a body and mind strong and clean and capable enough to express perfectly and consciously this Idea of Mine eternally working within his Soul.

Man, then, is only the organism I AM thus preparing through which to manifest the perfection of My Idea. He provides the personality, with its body, mind and intellect, through which I can express this Idea perfectly, the physical brain with which I can think and speak It into outer manifestation.

I plant in man's brain an Idea — any idea. That idea would grow, mature and speedily ripen into complete outer fruition or manifestation, — if man only would let it, would give his mind and all its thoughts, his heart and all its desires wholly over to Me, and let Me come forth as the perfect fulfillment of that Idea.

I will now plant in your brain-mind an Idea. May It grow, mature and ripen into the glorious harvest of Wisdom which is awaiting you, — if you *let Me* direct Its growth and expression through you.

In one of My other Revelations, called the Bible, you are told much about "The Word" but very few, even the most learned Bible students, comprehend My meaning.

You are told that:

"In the beginning was the Word, and the Word was with God, and the Word was God.

"The same was in the beginning with God.

All things were made by him, — by the Word, — and without Him — the Word — was not anything made that was made."

You shall learn herein *how* My Word was in the beginning, how It was *with* Me, and how It was *I*, My Self; how all things were made by Me and by My *Word*, and that without Me and My Word was nothing made that now exists.

Now, a word to the human understanding is a symbol of an Idea; that is, it stands for, embodies, and represents an Idea.

You are a Word, a symbol of an Idea, if you can see it. So is a diamond, a violet, a horse.

When you can discern the idea back of the symbol, then you know the soul or the reality of the manifestation *appearing* as a man, a diamond, a horse, a violet.

Hence, a word, as used in the above quotation, means an Idea, an Idea latent and unmanifest, however, waiting to be expressed, or thought and spoken forth, in some *form* or another.

The Word that was in the beginning and that was with Me was then not only an Idea, but It was *My Idea of My Self IN EXPRESSION* in a *new* state or condition, which you call earth life.

This Idea was I, My Self, because It was part of Me, being as yet latent and unmanifest within Me; for It was of the substance and essence of My *BE-ing*, which is Itself an Idea, the One Original Idea.

All things were made by Me by the vitalized action of this, My Idea, being thought and spoken into expression; and nothing has been or ever can be expressed in earth life without having My Idea as the primary and fundamental cause and principle of its being.

This, My Idea, therefore, is now in the *process* of unfoldment or of being thought into outer expression — some call it evolution, — just as is the flower when the bud puts forth from the stalk and finally opens into the blossom, obeying the urge to express My Idea hidden within its soul.

Just so will I develop and unfold all My mediums of expression, which shall finally, unitedly and completely picture forth My Idea from out their souls, in all the glory of Its perfection.

At present these mediums are of such nature that they require many languages of many types, from the simplest to the most complex, composed of almost an infinite number of Words, to express My Idea.

But when I shall have completely thought *out* My Idea, or shall have perfected My many mediums of expression, then shall My Idea shine forth in every Word, each, in fact, being a perfect part or phase of My

Idea, all so chosen and arranged that they will really be as *one* Word, radiating the sublime significance of My Meaning.

Then shall all languages have melted, merged, into one language, and all Words into One Word; for *all* mediums shall have become flesh, and all flesh shall have become One flesh, the *now perfected medium* for the complete expression *in One Word* of My Idea, — My SELF.

Then shall My SELF, now capable of being expressed by these perfected Words, shine through Its medium of expression, — through the personalities, their bodies, minds and intellects; and *the Word shall have become flesh, or shall BE the flesh.*

This means that all Words, through the regenerative power of My Idea within, shall have evolved *through* the flesh, transmuting and spiritualizing it and making it so transparent and pure that the personality will have nothing more of earth nature left in it to *hinder* Impersonal expression, enabling My SELF, therefore, to shine forth perfectly and become fully manifest; thus amalgamating once more all Words and all flesh into One Word, *THE WORD, which was in the beginning*, and which then will shine through all created flesh as the SUN OF GLORY, — The CHRIST of GOD!

This is the *plan* and *purpose* of My Creation and of all manifested things.

A glimpse of the *process* of My Creation, or of My Thinking My Idea of My Self into Earth expression, will be given in what follows.

VIII. MY IDEA

You have been told that the Earth and all things belonging to it are but the outer manifestations of My Idea, which is now in the *process* of being thought into perfect expression.

You have been shown that My Idea is responsible for all created things, and that It is both the Cause and the Reason for all manifestations, yourself and your brothers and sisters included, all of which have been thought into existence by Me, the One Original Thinker and Creator.

We will now trace the course of that Idea *from the beginning*, through Its various stages of Earth expression, as well as the process of My Thinking that Idea into its present state of manifestation.

In the beginning, at the dawn of a new Cosmic Day, when the Word consciousness was just awakening and the stillness of Cosmic Night yet prevailed, I The THINKER, conceived My Idea.

This My Idea of My Self in manifestation in a *new* condition, called Earth expression, I saw completely pictured in the mirror of My Omniscient Mind. In this mirror I saw the *real* Earth shining forth brilliantly in the Cosmos, — a perfect Sphere, where *all* the Infinite phases, attributes and powers of My Divine Nature were finding *perfect* expression through the medium of Angels of Light, living Messengers of My Will, My Word in the Flesh, even as It is in the Celestial World of the Eternal.

I saw My Self manifesting outwardly as Nature, and My Life as the vivifying and evolving Principle back of all Manifestation. I saw Love, the Divine Creative Power, as the animating and vitalizing Force back of all Life, and My Desire to give perfect expression to that Love as the Potential and Real Cause and Reason of the birth of My Idea.

All this I saw mirrored in My All-seeing and All-knowing Mind, which could see and reflect only the Soul of things or their Reality. Therefore this that I saw pictured in My Mind was the *Real* Earth, in fact, its *beginning*, its *conception* into Cosmic being.

Now, My Consciousness is the inner essence of all Space and all Life. It is the *real* Substance of My All-comprehending and All-including Mind, whose informing and vitalizing Center is everywhere and Its limit and circumference nowhere. *Within the realm of My Mind alone* I live and move and have My Being. It both contains and fills all things, and Its every vibration and manifestation is but the expression of some phase of My *Be-ing*.

Be-ing is ex-pressing or out-pressing. You cannot imagine be-ing without expression. Therefore, I, All that is, AM expressing, constantly and continuously expressing.

Expressing what?

What else could I express, if I AM All that Is, but My Self?

You cannot yet see or comprehend Me, My Self, but you can comprehend when I inspire you with an Idea.

Therefore, if I AM All there is, that Idea, *which is direct from Me*, must be part of or a phase of My Self in *Being* or Expression.

Any Idea, once born within the realm of *My Mind*, as has been shown, immediately becomes a Reality, for in the Eternality of My Being Time is not. With you, however, an Idea first creates Desire, a desire to express that Idea; then Desire compels Thinking, Thinking causes Action, and Action produces Results — the Idea in actual outer manifestation.

In Reality I have no Desire, for *I AM All Things*, and All Things are *of* Me. I need only to *think* and Speak the Word to produce results.

Yet that Desire you feel in you is from Me, because it is born of My Idea, which I implanted in your mind only that It might come forth into expression through you. Indeed, whatever you desire is I, knocking at the door of your mind, announcing My Purpose of manifesting My Self in you or through you in the particular form indicated by that Desire.

What is called Desire in human personalities, is but the necessary Action of My Will pushing forth the expression of My Idea into outer Manifestation or Being.

What to you would seem to be in Me a desire for expression, is but the *Necessity* of My Idea of My Self to *Be*, or Express Itself.

Therefore, every *real* desire you feel, every desire *of your heart,* comes from Me and must of necessity sometime, in some shape or other, be fulfilled.

However, as I have no Desire, because I AM All Things, once this Idea of expressing My Self in this new condition was born, I had but to *think*, that is, to concentrate or focus My Attention upon My Idea and Will It to come forth into expression, or, as is told in My other Revelation, to Speak the Creative Word, and at once did the Cosmic Forces of My BE-ing, set in vibration by the concentrating of My Will, proceed to attract the necessary elements from the eternal storehouse of My Mind, and, with My Idea as a nucleus, to combine, form and shape around It these elements into what is called a thought-form of a planet, filling it with My Life Substance — My Consciousness — and endowing it with all the potentialities of My Being.

This act of thinking produced only a vitalized *thought-form* of a planet, and its manifestation was still in a nebulous state in the thought realm.

From a thought-form, however, the quickening power of the Idea within, with My Will focused upon It, proceeded to mold, fashion and gradually to solidify into material form the various elements of Life

Substance; until My Idea finally shone forth in substantial manifestation in the world of visible forms as the planet Earth, a medium ready for living expression, and now capable of both containing and expressing Me.

This was the material body prepared by My Thinking, in which already dwelt all the *potential* nature of My Being, by reason of the informing power of My Idea within.

The next stage was the developing and preparing of avenues or mediums through which I could express the manifold phases, possibilities and powers of My Idea.

The outward evidence of this was what is known as the mineral, vegetable and animal kingdoms, which, each in turn, as it came into manifestation, gradually unfolded higher and more complex states of consciousness that enabled Me more and more clearly to express the infinite phases and variety of My Nature.

It was at this stage that I looked upon My Creation, as stated in My other Revelation, and saw that It was good;

But there yet remained the final and culminating medium of expression.

Up to this point, while each perfectly expressed some phase of My Nature, yet all existing mediums and avenues were unconscious of Me, and were mediums of expression only as a wire is a medium for conducting heat, light and power.

The conditions were ripe, however, for the creation of mediums through which *My Divine Attributes* could find *conscious* expression, conscious not only of their relationship to Me, but of their ability and power to express My Idea.

It was at this moment in Time that You and Your Brothers and Sisters were born into existence as human expressions, coming into manifestation as you did, similarly with all other mediums, in response to My concentrated Thought, in which I saw all the infinite variety of My Attributes in actual expression in entitized forms, each manifesting in predominance some particular phase of My Being, and each conscious of Me, Its Creator and Expressor.

I saw *You* in perfect expression, even as I see *You* now — the *Real* You, an *Attribute* of *My Self* — *perfect*.

For in Reality *You* are an Angel of Light, one of My Thought Rays, an Attribute of My Being, ensouled in Earth conditions, with no other purpose (which is no purpose at all, but a necessity of My Being) but the final complete expression of My Idea.

In the Eternal there is no Time, or Space, or Individuality, and it is only by reason of the phenomenon of Thought being born from the womb of Mind into the world of Matter that the illusions of Time, Space and Individuality occur; the thought, or Creature, acquiring the consciousness of separateness from its Thinker or Creator.

So it was then that the first tendency to *think* yourself as separate from Me was born. The complete consciousness of separation did not become established until long after.

In the beginning, when You thus first entered into Earth expression, obeying the impulse I had sent forth through My concentrated Thought, You, one of My Attributes, surrounded or clothed Your Self with *My Idea* of My Self in expression as the particular Attribute You represented. You being the animating Force of that Idea.

In other words, My Idea of My Self expressing that particular Attribute then became the *Soul* of Your particular expression. But that Idea or Soul is not You, remember, for You are really a part of Me, being My Self in expression through the medium of that particular Attribute.

Having clothed Your Self with My Idea, this Idea then, through the necessity of Its be-ing, immediately began to attract to Itself the necessary *Thought Substance* requisite for the *expression* of that particular Attribute, and to build and shape it into My Image and Likeness. It thus became a *Holy Temple*, filled with My living Presence, because inhabited by You, one of My Divine Attributes.

This Temple, being in My Image and Likeness, and composed of My Thought Substance, surrounding and clothing My Idea, is consequently your *Real* body. It is therefore indestructible, immortal, *perfect*. It is My complete, imagined (imaged in) Thought, containing My Living Essence, awaiting the time when it can come into outer expression and take on material form.

So now we have, —

First, *I AM*, expressing as *You*, one of My Divine Attributes;

Second, *My Idea* of You, one of My Attributes, expressing in Earth conditions — or *Your Soul*;

Third, *My Imaged Thought* of You, forming the Temple of Your Soul — or *Your Soul Body* in which You dwell.

These three make up the Divine or Impersonal part of You, the Immortal *Three-in-One* — You, My latent yet completely formulated thought, shaped in My Image and Likeness, as yet unquickened, and therefore having no connection with your human personality, which has not yet been born.

IX. THE GARDEN OF EDEN

Whether or not you have gotten any clear grasp of what has just been stated, do not discard it as impossible of comprehension. For in every line is hidden a meaning that will more than repay you for the study necessary to make it become clear.

This Message is to awaken you to a realization of what *You* are, to a realization of your *real* Self. It is intended to make you once more conscious of Me, your Divine Self, so conscious that never again will you be deceived by that other self, which you have imagined as being you and which so long has lured you on by feeding you with its unsatisfying sense pleasures, its mental dissipations and emotional delights.

Before that can be it will be necessary for you thoroughly to know that supposed other self, that self which You created by *thinking* it real and *separate* from Me, and then kept alive by giving it the power thus to entice and deceive you; yes, that self-created self, with its purely selfish pride and ambitions and imagined power, its love of life, of possessions, of being thought wise or good, — but which self is merely your human personality, which was born only to die as a separate identity, and as such has no more reality or permanence that the leaf, the snow or the cloud.

Yes, you will be brought face to face with that petty personal self, and will see with perfect vision all its sordid selfishness and human vanities; and you will then learn — if you but turn to Me and ask in simple faith and trust — that it is *I*, the Infinite, *Impersonal* part of You, abiding always *within*, Who am thus pointing out to you all these illusions of the personality, which for so many ages have separated you in consciousness from Me, Your glorious, Divine Self.

This realization will surely come, when you can recognize that this Message is from Me, and when you have determined that it shall be. To you, whom I have inspired with such a determination, I will cause *every* illusion in time to disappear, and you shall in truth *know* Me.

The exercise of your mind along these abstract lines will not hurt you. Instead it is what your mind needs. For, not until you can grasp My Meaning when presented to you in ideas such as are herein contained, coming from without, can you perceive and correctly interpret My Idea when I inspire you from within. Your mind I AM thus preparing for USE, not to gain more earthly knowledge, but in order that you can receive and *give forth* My Heavenly Knowledge to those whom I shall bring to you for that purpose.

With a prayer to Me, Your Own Real Self, your Father-in-Heaven, that true realization may come, read carefully what follows.

We have arrived, in the course of our consideration of the process of unfoldment of My Idea, to where the I AM of you, manifesting in your Immortal Soul Body, or in the Thought Image created by My Thinking, is now ready to take on a substantial form, a form suitable for the Earth expression of My Attributes.

This change from a mental to a mortal form took place after the manner and process of all thinking and creating, and is literally described in the Bible, where it says I "formed man of the dust of the ground, and breathed into his nostrils the breath of life; and man became a living soul."

Shall I explain further? — That the quickening power within My Idea (your Soul) proceeded to attract to it the various elements of life substance (dust), and, atom by atom, and cell by cell, in due course of time, to mold and shape each into substantial reality, after the pattern of the Thought Image composing your Soul Body, thus forming an Earthly outer covering, as it were, — until finally your mortal form actually became *manifest* to the psychic sense, if not yet to what is called the physical sense. Whereupon, all being now prepared for this cyclic moment, You, My Attribute, breathed into and then through its nostrils (from within) the breath of life, and *You* then made your first appearance on Earth as a *human being* — a *living* Soul (My Idea now able to express consciously through a suitable Earth medium), containing within your Self all of My Attributes, all of My Powers and all of My Possibilities.

Thus were now manifest all the various mediums for the Earth expression of My Idea; and You, being one of My Attributes, naturally had dominion over all of these mediums, or possessed the power of utilizing any or all of them, if necessary, for the full and complete expression of *Your* — My Attribute's — powers and possibilities.

In this manner and for this reason alone did You and Your Brothers and Sisters come into human expression. While in human form yet Your expression was so entirely Impersonal, that, though self-conscious, you still looked wholly to Me within for inspiration and guidance.

This, then, was the first condition into which You awakened when You entered into Earth expression, and is what is called the Edenic state or dwelling in the Garden of Eden.

This Edenic state represents the Celestial phase of Impersonal Consciousness, or that state in which You were still consciously One with Me, though now confined in a mortal medium of expression.

Now, I shall not tell you in detail how or why it became necessary for Me to "drive" You (now manifesting as Man or Humanity) out of the Garden of Eden, other than to remind you of the part that Desire plays in Earth expression, and its relation to My Will; how it centers your interest in outer things and makes you forget Me within.

When you have solved that and comprehended somewhat of My reason, then perhaps you can understand the necessity of first causing You (Humanity) to fall into a deep sleep (You having arrived at the close of another Cycle called a Cosmic day), and of letting you dream you had awakened, — but in reality you were *and are still* asleep, and everything from that day to this, including all seeming earthly events and conditions, have been but a Dream, from which you will fully awaken only when You (Humanity) again become wholly conscious of Me within, — and of finding Yourself (Humanity) no longer outwardly one, but two; one an active, thinking, aggressive part, thereafter called a man, and the other a passive, feeling, receptive part, — a womb-man, or woman;

Also the necessity of these seeming earth influences being brought to bear to draw Your consciousness from purely Celestial delights and to hold it in this new Dream condition, in order to develop a mortal mind, that You might through its natural selfish tendencies become centered entirely upon Your Earthly mission of mortal expression;

And the wisdom of having this influence, through the Serpent of Selfishness (the shape I caused it to assume in your mind), first generate in the passive, feeling, receptive part of You — *Desire*, the mortal agent of My Will, which was to supply the motives and the power for the further and complete expression of My Attributes on Earth;

And finally the necessity of Desire casting its complete spell over You (Humanity), that Your Celestial or Impersonal nature might be kept deep in sleep; until, in your Dream, by the free but ignorant use of My Will, You could taste and fully eat of the *fruit* of the so-called Tree of Knowledge of Good and Evil, and through the eating could learn properly to discriminate and know its fruit for what it really is; and thus acquire the strength to use the knowledge thus gained wisely and perfectly in the expression of My Idea only.

You likewise possibly now can understand how in your Dream you became more and more engrossed in and attached to this false earth state, through first eating of this fruit and learning to know Good *and* Evil, and after learning of the new and enticing world thus opened up to you, dying to the knowledge of the Reality back of it all; and how and why it was You learned that You were naked — both the thinking and the feeling parts of You; and also why you grew afraid and tried to hide from Me, thus creating in your consciousness the sense of separation from Me.

Now, perhaps, you can see why this all had to be, why You (Humanity) had to leave the Edenic state of Impersonal Consciousness and lose Your Self wholly in the earth illusions of this Dream World, in order to be able to create a body and develop in it a personal or self consciousness capable of fully expressing My Perfection.

Thus was born Your human personality, and since its birth have I impelled You to nourish, support and strengthen it, by filling You with longings, hopes, ambitions, and aspirations, with *all* the various manifestations of Desire; which are but the human phases of My Will, operating in the preparation and development of a medium capable of expressing perfectly My Attributes on Earth.

And so I Spake the Word, and drove You out of the Garden of Eden, and clothed You with a "coat of skin," or, in other words, with flesh, the same as other animals. For now, in order that You might enter into the heart of Earth conditions, into the *real* Earth, the Earth of My Idea, — not the one of your Dream, — so as to quicken My Idea therein into active *life* expression, You, My Attribute, had to have an organism and a covering appropriate to the conditions in which You were to manifest in your Dream.

Likewise, in thus giving You a coat of skin, did I, by so doing, provide My Idea with a suitable form for Earthly expression, — I gave you the power to express Your Self, through a definite organism, by means of words.

In the Impersonal there is no use or necessity for words. Ideas alone exist and express. They simply *Are*, for they are the expression of the various phases of My *Be-ing*.

But in this Dream condition, where every expression in these early stages of outer being had to have a form and substance that could be heard, seen, felt, smelled or tasted, in order that its meaning could be clearly apprehended, there naturally had to be provided organisms capable of being used for the double purpose of expression and of understanding what was expressed.

As My Idea unfolded Itself, after Your expulsion from Eden, You — one of My Divine Attributes, dwelling within My Idea of that Attribute in expression, in turn dwelling within the Thought Image of My Self, and finally manifesting outwardly in the Earth form of Words, when impelled by My Will in the guise of Desire to express My Meaning — began rapidly to "increase and multiply."

In Your search for the most favorable conditions for the manifestation of Your particular attributes, You gradually spread over the face of the Earth, quickening and arousing the Intelligence dormant in all forms of life contacted into fuller and more active expression of their particular phases of My Idea.

Thus were formed the various Languages of Earth, each containing many words, and all born of Desire in the human mind to express in Earthly terms the infinite phases of My Idea ever surging within.

The more the *human* mind strove thus to express — in Words — My Idea, the greater and more abject the failure.

In time will the Great Awakening come — that all Words are but Symbols of One Idea, and all Ideas of whatsoever nature are but phases of One Idea, My Idea of My Self in Expression, — and that all Desire to express in Words that Idea, without the consciousness of My Will being the One and Only source of Inspiration, is futile. Likewise, all desire to express that Idea in *living acts*, without losing all consciousness of your human personality — of your personal part in the acts, and centering your self wholly in Me, — is vain and fruitless and will end only in failure, disappointment and humiliation.

X. GOOD AND EVIL

In the Garden of Eden, where you abode before entering upon your Earthly mission, there grew this tree whose fruit is called the Knowledge of Good and Evil.

While dwelling in the Garden you were still wholly Impersonal, for you had not yet tasted of this fruit. Having once yielded to Desire, the Earthly agent of My Will, whose main work is to make you eat this fruit, the moment you had eaten, that moment you descended, or fell, or were forced from your Edenic estate (like the chick from the shell or the rose from the bud), and you found yourself involved in conditions altogether new and strange. For now, instead of having dominion over the lower kingdoms, and of their supplying your every want, you had to till the ground to get it to bring forth fruit, and by the sweat of your brow had you to earn your bread.

Having taken upon yourself this Earthly mission, it now became necessary for you to enter fully into all conditions of Earth life, in order to develop a mind and perfect a body capable of expressing perfectly My Idea on Earth, — the real cause and reason of your entering into this Dream condition.

So having fallen or stepped out of your Impersonal or Edenic estate, you yielded completely to the lure of this Dream World, and now permitting Desire wholly to lead, you no longer were capable of seeing the Reality or Soul of things; for you had put on a physical body, an earthly covering with a human brain, which acted as a veil to your Soul Consciousness, and so bedimmed your sight and clouded your mind that the light of Truth did not penetrate through, and everything was falsely colored and distorted by your human understanding.

In this Dream condition you saw all things darkly, as through a mist, and with this mist enshrouding everything you could not see things in their Reality, but only their misty *appearance*, which now however seemed to you the *real* things themselves.

This was so with everything you saw through your Dream eyes, with things both animate and inanimate, with everything you conceived in your human mind, with even your own Self and your other Selves round about you.

Thus no longer seeing the Soul of things, but only their misty shadows, you grew to thinking these shadows were real substance, and that the world about you was composed of and filled with such substance.

This mist was only the effect of the Light of Truth being invisible to your human mind, whose intellect, like an imperfect lens, only befogged and twisted everything and made it *appear* as Real, keeping your consciousness continually busied with these myriad illusions of your Dream World.

Now the intellect is a creature of and wholly controlled by Desire, and is not, as many suppose, a faculty of the Soul. In other words, this mist then was the clouded lens of your human intellect, which, because controlled by Desire, falsely portrayed and interpreted to your consciousness every image, idea and impulse I inspired from within or attracted from without, during the process of My awakening your consciousness to a recognition of My Idea within ever urging for outer expression.

All this I did purposely, however, through the agency of Desire, in order to lead you consciously into the heart of Earth conditions.

While this false vision, inspired by Desire, caused many mis-steps and much trouble and suffering, and you gradually lost confidence in your Self — in Me, the Impersonal One within, — in fact, you forgot Me, so that you did not know where to turn in your helplessness; yet it was only through your thus losing the memory of your Divine estate, and centering *all* your consciousness in these earthly conditions, that I could develop your human mind and will, and all your faculties, and provide your human body with the strength and powers that would enable Me to give perfect expression to My Divine Idea on Earth, which eventually must BE.

So, through your mistakes and troubles and sufferings, Desire for relief caused the Idea of Evil to spring up in your mind, and likewise when these troubles were not It inspired the Idea of Good.

To all *appearances* of things and conditions you attributed these qualities of Good or Evil, — according to whether or not they satisfied Desire My Agent, in Reality My *human Self*, or *You*, in your human personality.

All these conditions and experiences in life which you entered into, and which when pleasing seemed Good, and when displeasing seemed Evil, were merely incidents created by Desire to quicken in you certain Soul faculties, which would enable you to recognize the Truths that I, within, wished at the time to impress upon your consciousness. The apparent Evil was the negative aspect of the Fruit of the Tree, which always lured you on by its fair appearance and by the sweetness of the first taste to eat and enjoy to satiation, or until its harmful effects manifested and became a curse, bringing final disillusionment; which served to turn or force you back in humiliation to Me, your True Self, Who, through the new consciousness thus aroused, was then enabled to extract the Essence of the Fruit and incorporate it into Soul substance and tissue.

Likewise the apparent Good was the positive aspect of the Fruit, which, having pushed forth of itself into expression, through your recognition of and obedience to its urge, was now permitting you to enjoy its happy and natural *effects,* and to receive the outward benefits of *My* loving inspiration and guidance.

This *you,* who was being led by Desire through all these experiences, was only your human personality, which the *Real* you was training and developing and preparing so it could become a perfect instrument for Your *use* in the expression of My Idea, ever seeking to manifest Its perfection in the flesh.

All this *You* did, not only compelling your human personality to eat but to *live* on the *fruit* of the so-called Tree of Knowledge of Good and Evil, until you had seen and known *all* the so-called Evil, and from living *on* and *with* it had discovered *in* it the germ of so-called Good, plucked it, lifted it up, and turned it right-side out; so that you from that time on knew that Good and Evil had no real existence, and were but relative terms descriptive of *outside* conditions looked at from different viewpoints, or were only different outer aspects of a central *inner* Truth, the *Reality* of which was what *You* sought to Know, Be and Express.

During the latter ages you have been, as it were, gradually throwing off layer after layer of human consciousness, dissipating the mist or glamour thrown around your mind by the intellect; subduing, controlling, spiritualizing, and thus clarifying the intellect itself; until now you are beginning to awaken and to see, through the ever thinning remaining layers, occasional glimpses of Me, the one Great Reality, within all things.

All this time, *You,* the omniscient, Impersonal I AM of You, were consciously and intentionally doing all this; not for the purpose of getting the mere knowledge of earth conditions and things, as your

Intellect has so loudly and authoritatively proclaimed, but in order that you might harvest what You had sown in the dim ages past, and could manifest My Perfect Idea on Earth, even as You are now manifesting It in the Impersonal estate, Your Heavenly Home.

You, remember, are the Great Impersonal I, Who AM doing all this, Who AM continually changing in outward appearance, but Who within AM eternally the same.

The endless flow of the Seasons, — the Spring, with its busy sowing; the Summer, with its warm, restful ripening; the Autumn, with its bounteous harvesting; the Winter, with its cool, peaceful plenty, year after year, life after life, century after century, age after age — are only the outbreathing of My Idea as I inspire It forth through the Earth and through You, My Attribute, and through all My other Attributes, during the process of unfolding in outer manifest state the perfection of My Nature.

Yes, I am doing it through You, because You are an expression of Me, because only through You, My Attribute, can I express My Self, can I BE. I AM because You Are. You ARE because I AM expressing My SELF.

I AM in You as the oak is in the acorn. You are I as the sunbeam is the Sun. You are a phase of Me in expression. You, one of My Divine Attributes, are eternally trying to express My perfection through Your mortal personality.

Just as an artist sees in his mind the perfect picture he wants to paint, but his hand cannot quite portray with the crude mediums of brush and color the true quality and effect he sees, so do You see Me within Your Self and know We are One, but always are prevented, by the imperfection of the earthly material of your human personality, with its animal body, its mortal mind, and selfish intellect, from perfectly expressing Me.

Yet, I created your body, mind and intellect, in order to express My Self through you. The body I made in the Image of My Perfection; the mind I gave to inform you of Me and My works; the intellect I gave to interpret My Idea as I inspired it to the mind. But you have been so distracted by the *human* phases of this body, mind and intellect, and their outer uses, that you have forgotten Me, the One and Only Reality within, Whose Divine nature I AM ever seeking to express to and through you.

The time is soon here when the outward uses shall no longer distract, and My Reality shall be revealed unto you in all the glory of Its perfection *within* You.

You, when I thus reveal My Self, shall not be more blessed than before, unless that which I have revealed shall become the Bread of Life to you, and you shall live and *manifest* the Life It reveals.

XI. USE

Now I have purposely not stated clearly all the how and why of these things; for I have reserved for you, when you call upon Me so to do, and are capable of receiving it, an inspiration *from within* with a far more comprehensive vision of the unfoldment and development of My Divine Idea, and Its final perfected expression, than is herein pictured.

If I were here to tell the *real* meaning of My many manifestations, before you were consciously capable of experiencing its Truth, you neither would believe My words, nor could you comprehend their inner application and use.

Therefore, as I begin to awaken in you a realization that I AM within, and more and more cause your human consciousness to become an Impersonal channel through which I can express, will I gradually reveal to you the Reality of My Idea, dissipating one by one the illusions of the ages which have hidden Me from you, enabling Me thereby to manifest through you My Heavenly Attributes on Earth in all their humanly Divine perfection.

I have herein given you but a glimpse of My Reality, but just to the extent that that which has been revealed becomes clear will more be opened up unto you from *within*, and far more wonderful than this now seems to you.

For My Idea within, when It finally and completely shines through Its mantle of flesh, will compel you to worship and glorify Me far above all that your human mind and intellect now conceive of as God.

Before you can become conscious of all this and can truly comprehend it, you and your human personality must make it possible for Me to reveal it, by turning within to Me as the *One* and *Only* Source, bringing to Me your measure absolutely empty of self, and with mind and heart as simple and trusting as those of a child.

Then and then only, when nothing of the personal consciousness remains to prevent My filling you full to overflowing with the consciousness of Me, can I point out to you the glories of My Real Meaning, for which this whole Message is but the outer preparation.

The time has now arrived, however, for you to comprehend somewhat of this. Enough has been revealed to prepare you for the recognition of My Voice speaking within.

Therefore, I shall now proceed as if you realize I AM within, and that these Truths which I voice through the medium of these pages are but to impress more strongly upon your consciousness those phases of My Idea which you could not clearly receive direct.

That which herein appeals to you as Truth is consequently but a confirmation of that which My Idea has heretofore been struggling to express from within.

That which does not appeal and which you do not recognize as your own, pass by, for that means I do not desire you to receive it as yet.

But each Truth I voice herein will go on vibrating until It reaches the minds I have quickened to receive It; for every word is filled with the potent power of My Idea, and to minds that perceive the Truth hidden therein this Truth becomes a living Reality, being that phase of My Idea they are now worthy and capable of *expressing*.

As all minds are but phases of My Infinite Mind, or parts of It manifesting in different forms of mortal nature, when I speak through the medium of these pages to your mind and to other minds, I AM but speaking to My mortal Self, thinking with My Infinite Mind, pushing forth My Idea into earthly expression.

Just so will *You* soon be thinking *My* Thoughts, and be conscious that I AM speaking within directly to your human consciousness, and you will then no longer have to come to this or to any other of My *outer* Revelations, either spoken or written, in order to perceive My Meaning.

For AM I not within You, and AM I not You, and are You not One with Me, Who live in and express through the consciousness of all minds, knowing all things?

All that remains for you to do is to enter into the All-consciousness of My Mind and abide there with Me, even as I abide within My Idea in Your Mind. Then all things shall be Yours, as they now are Mine, being but the outer *expression* of My Idea, and existing only by reason of the consciousness I gave them when I thought them into being.

It is all a matter of consciousness — of your conscious thinking. You are separated from Me only because you *think* you are. Your mind is but a focal point of My Mind. If you but knew it, what you call *your* consciousness is My Consciousness. You cannot even think, much less breathe or exist without *My* Consciousness being in you, — Can you not see it?

Well, then, *think*, *believe* you are I, that We are not separated, that We could not possibly be separated; for WE are ONE, — I within You, and You within Me, Think this is so; determinedly *image* it as so; and verily the moment you *are conscious* of this, that moment are you with Me in Heaven.

You are what you *believe* you are. Not one thing in your life is Real or has any value to you only as your *thinking* and *believing* has made it such.

Therefore, *think* no more you are separated from Me, and abide *with* Me in the Impersonal Realm, where all Power, all Wisdom, and all Love, the threefold nature of My Idea, but await expression through You.

Now I have spoken much of this, and have apparently said the same thing more than once, but in different words. I have done this purposely, presenting My Meaning in different lights, that you might finally be brought to comprehend My Divine Impersonality, which is in Reality *Your* Impersonality.

Yes, I have repeated and will continue to repeat many Truths, and you may think it tedious and unnecessary; but if you will read carefully you will find that each time I repeat a Truth I always add something to what has already been said, and that each time a stronger and more lasting impression is made upon your mind.

This done, My purpose has been accomplished, and you will soon come into a *Soul* realization of that Truth.

If you receive not such impression and still think such repetition a useless waste of words and time, know that your intellect only is reading, and that My *real* meaning has altogether escaped you.

You, however, who do comprehend, will love every word, and will read and re-read many times, and consequently will receive all the wondrous Pearls of Wisdom I have held in reserve for you.

This book and its message will be to you hereafter merely a fount of inspiration, or a door through which you will be enabled to enter into the Impersonal estate and to hold sweet communion with Me, your Father in Heaven, when I will teach you all things you desire to know.

I have been picturing the Impersonal estate from many viewpoints, in order that it may become so familiar that you can unerringly distinguish it from all inferior states, and may learn to dwell consciously in it at will.

When you can consciously dwell in it so that My Words when and wherever spoken can always find lodgment and understanding in your mind, then will I permit you to *use* certain faculties I have been awakening in you. These faculties will enable you more and more clearly to see the Reality of things, not only the beautiful and lovely qualities in the personalities of those about you, but their weaknesses, faults and shortcomings, as well.

But the reason you are enabled to see these faults and shortcomings, is not that you may criticize or judge your brother, but that I may arouse in you a definite resolve to overcome such faults and shortcomings in your own personality. For, mark you! — You would take no note of them in others were they not still in your self; for I within, then would not need to call them to your attention.

As all things are for *use*, and *use* only, let us study the use you have hitherto made of other faculties, gifts and powers I have given you.

You must realize by this time *I* have allowed you *all things*. All you have, or are, be it of good or evil, of blessing or suffering, of success or failure, of riches or lack, *I* have allowed you or attracted to you. — Why? For USE — in awakening you to a recognition and acknowledgment of *Me* as The Giver of All that is Good.

Yes, all things you receive have their use. If you are not conscious of such use, it is only because you can not yet acknowledge Me as The Giver.

You could not honestly acknowledge Me as such until you *knew* I AM, The Giver. Your personality, in fact, had become so engrossed in trying to get rid of or to exchange many of the things I had given you for other things you thought were better, that of course you could not even dream, much less acknowledge, Me, *Your Own Self*, as The Giver.

Possibly you do now acknowledge Me as The Giver, as the Inner Essence and Creator of all things in your world and in your life, even of your present attitude toward these things.

Both are My doing, for they are but the outer phases of the process I AM using in the expression of My Idea of your inner Perfection, which Perfection being My Perfection is gradually unfolding from within you.

As you more and more realize this, will the true meaning and *use* of the things, conditions and experiences I send be revealed unto you. For you will then begin to glimpse My Idea within, and when you glimpse that Idea will you begin to *know* Me — your own *Real* Self.

Before you can truly know Me, however, you must learn that *all* things I give you are *Good* — and that they are for *use*, My use, — and that you personally have no interest in or actual right to them, and they are of no real benefit to you, only as you put them to such use.

I may be expressing through you beautiful symphonies of sound, color or language, that manifest as music, art or poetry, according to human terminology, and which so affect others as to cause them to acclaim you as one of the great ones of the day.

I may be speaking through your mouth or inspiring you to write many beautiful Truths, which may be attracting to you many followers, who hail you as a most wonderful preacher or teacher.

I may even be healing through you divers diseases, casting out devils, making the blind to see and the lame to walk, and performing other marvelous works which the world calls miracles.

Yes, all these I may be doing through you, but of absolutely no benefit is any of it to you personally, unless you use and apply these harmonies of sound in your every spoken word, so that to all hearers they will seem as the sweet music of heaven; and unless your sense of color and proportion so manifests in your life that only kind, uplifting, helpful thoughts flow from you, proving that the only true art is that of seeing clearly My Perfection in all My human expressions, and of allowing the quickening power of My Love to pour through you into their hearts, picturing to *their* inner vision My Image hidden therein.

Likewise no credit attaches to you, no matter what wonderful Truths I speak or works I perform through you, unless you, yourself, *live* these Truths, daily, hourly; and make these works serve as a constant reminder of Me and My Power, which I ever pour out freely for you, My Beloved, and for all, to use in My Service.

You, to whom I have apparently given none of such gifts and who deem yourself unworthy and not yet advanced enough to serve Me in such ways, — to you I would say:

Just to the extent that you truly recognize Me within and seek in real earnestness to serve Me, just to that extent will I use you — no matter what your personality, no matter what its faults, tendencies and weaknesses.

Yes, I will cause even you who thus seek to serve Me to do many wondrous things towards the quickening and awakening of your brothers to a like acknowledgment of Me. I will cause even you to influence and affect the lives of many of those whom you contact, inspiring and uplifting them to higher ideals, changing their way of thinking and their attitude towards their fellows and therefore towards Me.

Yes, *all you* who seek to serve Me, no matter what your gifts, will I make to be a vital force for good in the community, altering the mode of life of many, inspiring and molding their ambitions and aspirations, and altogether becoming a leavening influence in the midst of the worldly activities in which I will place you.

You at the time will probably know nothing of this. You may even be still longing to serve Me, and hungering for a more intimate consciousness of Me, thinking you are doing nothing, are still making many mistakes and failing to live up to your highest ideals of Me; not realizing that this longing and hungering is the avenue through which I pour forth My Spiritual Power, which being wholly Impersonal, is used by you, unconscious of its being *I within you* using it, to bring about My Purpose in your heart and life and in the hearts and lives of My and Your other Selves.

So, as you finally grow into the realization of all this, as you surely will, and *prove* it by the practical *use* of all you have in *My* service, will I gradually give you the strength and ability consciously to use *Impersonally My* Power, *My* Wisdom, and *My* Love, in the expression of My Divine Idea, which is eternally striving to manifest through You Its Perfection.

Therefore will you soon see that your human personality, with all its faculties, powers and possessions, which are in reality Mine operating and manifesting through you, is likewise for My use wholly, and that true success and satisfaction can never be found except in such use.

For such use develops, as the planted seed develops the harvest, the ability consciously to use *all* My spiritual faculties in the final perfect expression of My Idea, which can be expressed only through your human personality.

XII. SOUL MATES

Let us now examine into some of the things I have given you, those especially of which you cannot yet acknowledge Me as the Giver.

Perhaps the particular position in life you now occupy you do not think the best adapted for the expression of My Idea surging within you.

If so, then why not step out of that position into the one of *your* choice?

The mere fact that you cannot or do not do this proves that at this time such position is the one best suited to awaken in you certain qualities necessary for My perfect expression, and that I, your own Self, AM permitting you to remain therein, until you can recognize my Purpose and Meaning hidden within the power such position has to disturb your peace of mind and keep you thus dissatisfied.

When you recognize My Meaning and determine to make My Purpose your purpose, then and then only will I give you the strength to step out of that position into a higher I have provided for you.

Perhaps the husband or the wife you have, you think is far from being suited to you or capable of helping along your "spiritual" awakening, being only a hindrance and detriment, instead. You may even be secretly contemplating leaving or wishing you could leave that one for another who sympathizes and joins with you in your aspirations and seeking, and therefore seems more nearly your ideal.

You may run away if you will, but know that you cannot run away from your own personality; that, in selfish craving for a "spiritual" mate you may attract only one who will force you to a tenfold longer and harder search among the illusions of the mind, before you can again awaken to the consciousness of My Voice speaking within.

For a sympathetic and appreciative mate would only feed the personal pride and selfish desire for "spiritual" power in you, and develop further the egotistic side of your nature. Likewise, a loving, trusting, yielding mate might encourage only selfishness and conceit, when you are not yet abiding in the consciousness of My Impersonal

Love; while a tyrannical, suspicious, nagging mate may provide the soul discipline you still need.

Did you but know it, the one who is your true Soul mate is in reality an Angel from Heaven, even as are You, one of the Attributes of My Divine Self, come to you to teach you that only when you have purged your own personality so that My Holy Love can express, can you be freed from any conditions which may now be causing you so much disturbance of mind and unhappiness of Soul.

For not until this Soul, this Angel from Heaven, this other part of My and Your Self, who has come to you and is yearning and striving to call into expression through you the Impersonal Love, the tender, thoughtful care for others, the poise of mind and peace of heart, the quiet, firm mastery of self, which and which alone can open the doors, so It can step forth into the freedom of Its own glorious Being and be to you Its own *true* Self, — not until you can see this Soul in all Its Divine beauty, free of this earthly bondage, will it ever be possible for you to find and recognize that Ideal you seek.

For that Ideal exists, not without — in some other personality, — but only within, in your Divine Counterpart, which is I, your Higher, Immortal Self. It is only My *Idea* of this, your Perfect Self, striving to express and become manifest through your personality, that causes you to see seeming imperfections in the mate I have given you.

The time will come, however, when you cease to look without for love and sympathy, appreciation and spiritual help, and turn wholly to Me within, that these seeming imperfections will disappear; and you will see in this mate only the *reflection* of qualities of unselfish love, gentleness, trust, a constant endeavor to make the other happy, that will then be shining brightly and continuously from out your own heart.

Perhaps you cannot yet wholly believe all this, and you still question that I, your own Self, am responsible for your present position in life, or that I chose for you your present mate?

If so, it is well for you thus to question until all is made plain.

But remember, I will speak much more clearly *direct* from within, if you but turn trustingly to Me for help. For I ever preserve My Holiest secrets for those who turn to Me in deep, abiding Faith that I can and will supply their every need.

To you, however, who cannot yet do this, I say, if your own Self did not place you here or provide this mate, *Why* then are you here? and *Why* have you this mate?

Think!

I, the ALL, the Perfect One, make no mistake.

Yes, but the personality does, you say. And the personality chose this mate, and perhaps has *earned* no better position.

What, *who*, caused the personality to choose this particular one and earn this particular position in life? *Who* picked out and placed this one where you could thus choose, and who caused you to be born in this country of all countries and in this town of all towns in the world at this particular time? Why not some other town and a hundred years later? Did your personality do all these things?

Answer truly and satisfactorily these questions to yourself, and you will learn that I God, within you, your own Self, do all things that you do, and I do them well.

I do them while expressing My Idea, Which is ever seeking manifestation in outer form as *Perfection* through you, My living Attribute, even as it is in the Eternal, within.

As for your true "Soul Mate," which you have been led by others to believe must be waiting for you somewhere, cease looking; for it exists not without in some other body, but within your own Soul.

For that within you which cries out for completion is only your sense of Me within, yearning for recognition and expression; Me, your own Divine Counterpart, the Spiritual part of you, your other half, to which and which alone you must be united, before you can finish what you came on Earth to express.

This is indeed a mystery to you who are not yet wedded in consciousness to your Impersonal Self; but doubt not, when you can come to Me in complete surrender, and will care for naught else than union with Me, then will I disclose to you the sweets of the Celestial Ecstasy I have long kept in reserve for you.

XIII. AUTHORITY

To you who still feel the desire to read books, thinking in them to find an explanation of the mysteries that now hide from you the meaning of the earthly expressions of My Idea, I say:

It is well that you seek thus outwardly, following the impulses I send, for others' interpretations of the meaning My Idea is expressing through them; for I will make that search to be of benefit to you, though not in the way you imagine.

It is even well for you to seek in ancient teachings, philosophies and religions, or in those of other races and other peoples, for the Truth I wish to express to you; for even that search will prove not unprofitable.

But the time will come when you will realize that the thoughts of other minds and the teachings of other religions, no matter how true and beautiful, are not what I intend for you; for I have reserved for you thoughts and teachings which are yours and yours only, and which I will give to you in secret — when you are ready to receive them.

When the time comes, as it inevitably will, that you become dissatisfied in your search among the teachings of the various religions, philosophies and cults that now are interesting you, and you grow discouraged at finding yourself no nearer the attainment of the powers and spiritual growth so authoritatively described and supposedly possessed by the writers of the books, the teachers of the philosophies and the promulgators of the religions, — then will I show you that while all these books, teachings and religions were originally inspired by Me, and have done and are still doing their part in quickening the hearts of many, yet for *you* it is now meant that you cease looking to *any outer* authority, and instead confine your study to My Book of Life, guided and instructed by Me within, by Me alone. If you earnestly and truly do this, you will find that I have chosen you to be the High Priest of a religion, the glory and grandeur of which will be to all others that have been pictured to your former understanding, as the light of the Sun is to the twinkle of the far distant star.

You will likewise realize that the ancient religions were given to My peoples of long ages past, and that the religions of other races are for My peoples of those races, and that none of these are for you; even though I brought them to you and pointed out many wondrous things in them that inspired you to a more determined search for Me within their teachings.

I say to you, these are things of the past and have naught to do with you. The time has arrived, if you can see it, when you must cast aside all accumulated knowledge, all teachings, all religions, all authority, even My authority as expressed in this and My other *outer* revelations; for I have quickened you to the consciousness of My Presence *within*, to the fact that all authority, teachings and religions, coming from any *outer* source, no matter how lofty or sacred, can no longer have any influence with you, except as they become a means of turning you within to Me, for My *final* authority on all questions of whatsoever nature.

Therefore, why seek in the things of the past — in religion, human knowledge, or in others' experiences — for the help and guidance which I alone can give?

Forget all that has gone before. That which is past is dead. Why burden your soul with dead things?

Just to the extent you hold to things that are past, do you still live in the past, and can have naught to do with Me, Who dwell in the ever-present NOW, the Eternal.

Just to the extent you attach yourself to past acts or experiences, religions or teachings, do they cloud your soul vision, hiding Me from you. They will ever prevent your finding Me until you free yourself of their darkening influence and step within, into the Light of My Impersonal Consciousness, which recognizes no limitations and penetrates to the infinite Reality of all things.

Likewise the future concerns *you* not. He who looks to the future for his final perfection is chained to the past and can never get free, until his mind no longer is thus engrossed with the consequences of his acts, and he recognizes Me as his only Guide and throws all responsibility upon Me.

You, who are one with Me, are perfect *now*, and always were perfect, knowing neither youth nor old age, birth nor death.

You, the Perfect, have naught to do with what has been or what is to be. You care not for anything but the eternal *NOW*. That only concerns you which immediately confronts you, — how perfectly to express My Idea here and now in the condition in which I have placed you purposely for such expression.

When that has been done, why not leave it behind, instead of dragging it along with you, burdening your mind and soul with consequences which are but empty shells from which you have extracted the meat?

All this applies to reincarnation, to which belief many minds are fast chained.

What have You, the Perfect, the Eternal, to do with past or future incarnations? Can the Perfect add to Its perfection? Or the Eternal come out of or return to eternity?

I AM, and You Are, — ONE with Me, — and always have been, and always will be. The I AM of You dwells in and reincarnates in ALL bodies, for the one purpose of expressing My Idea.

Humanity is My Body. In It I live, move and have My Being, expressing the Glorious Light of My Idea through My Attributes, whose Celestial Radiance to the human vision is bedimmed and distorted by the myriads of clouded and imperfect facets of the human intellect.

I and You, Who are One with Me, reincarnate in Humanity, as the oak reincarnates in its leaves and acorns, season after season, and again in the thousand oaks born from their thousands of acorns and their oaks, generation after generation.

You say you remember your past lives.

Do you? Are you *sure?*

Very well, what if you do? Just because I have permitted you a glimpse of the Reality of one of My past Expressions, that you might the better comprehend My Meaning which I am *now* expressing to you, is no assurance from *Me* that you *personally* were My Avenue of that expression.

For do I not express through all avenues, and You with Me, and are We not the Life and Intelligence of all expression, no matter what the character, or the age, or race?

If it pleases you to believe that *you* actually were that expression, it is well, and I shall cause such belief to be of benefit to you; but only to the extent of preparing you for the great Realization that afterward will come.

In the meantime you are chained fast. Your personality, with its selfish desires and selfish seeking, is still bound hand and foot to the past, and looks only to the future for its deliverance, after the final wearing out of all the consequences of its acts; dominating your mind and intellect with this false belief in birth and death, and that such is *your* only way to final emancipation and union with Me; preventing the realization of Our Eternal and Ever-Constant Oneness, and that You can free your Self any moment You will.

For it is only the personality that is born and dies, and which seeks and strives to prolong its stay in the body and in earth life, and then to return to other bodies after I no longer have any use for its body.

It is only to this personality that you are bound, by the benefits and opinions it has engrafted on you back through the ages, during which it has kept your human mind busied with such delusions. It is only when you can rise up in the realization of your Divine Immortality, Omnipotence and Intelligence, and can cast off *all* personal beliefs and opinions, that you can free your Self from this perverted relation, and can assume your true position as Master and King, One with Me, seated upon the Throne of SELF, compelling the personality to take its proper and natural place as servant and subject, ready and willing to obey My slightest command, thereby becoming an instrument worthy of My Use.

XIV. MEDIUMS AND MEDIATORS

You, who, in your desire to serve Me, have joined yourself with a church, religious organization, occult society, or spiritual order, of whatsoever nature, thinking, by aiding in and supporting its work, it would please Me, and that you might receive special favors from Me in consequence, — harken to these My Words and ponder over them.

First, know that I AM already pleased with you, for you do nothing that I do not cause you to do, and you do it to fulfill My Purpose, — although it may seem to you at times you are acting contrary to My Wish and only to satisfy your own desires.

Know likewise that I provide all minds with all their experiences of life, which I utilize solely to prepare the body, quicken the heart and develop the consciousness, so that they can comprehend Me, and so that I can express through them My Idea.

I inspire minds with glimpses of Me and My Idea through these experiences, and I have spoken thus through inspiration to many, who have taken My Words and have written them in books and have taught them to other minds. These Words I have caused to quicken the hearts and consciousness of those who are ready to receive them, even though the writers and teachers of themselves had no real comprehension of My Meaning.

Many of those whose minds I thus inspire with glimpses of Me and My Idea I cause to become teachers and leaders, organizing churches and societies and cults, drawing seekers and followers to them, that I, through the words I speak through them, can quicken the hearts and consciousness of those that are ready to recognize Me.

I, the Impersonal One within, do all this, and the teachers and leaders personally do nothing, only serving as channels through which My Idea can express to the consciousness of those I draw to them for that purpose.

For the mind is only a channel and the intellect an instrument, which I use Impersonally wherever and whenever necessary to express My Idea. Not until the *heart* has been quickened and has opened wide to contain Me can man, with his mortal mind and intellect, consciously comprehend My Meaning, when I express through him My Idea.

You, in your desire to serve Me, may have found in some teacher or leader a personality whom you think, from the many seemingly wondrous words I speak through him, is now containing Me in his heart.

In your doubts and anxiety to please Me, and in your fear of My displeasure when disobeying My Commands, you may even have gone to such teacher or leader, who possibly claimed to be a priest or priestess of the Most High, thinking to get through such My Message to you, or words of advice or help from some "Master" or "Guide" you can hold. Until finally, in sorrow and humiliation from the disillusionment of which eventually and inevitably follows, you once more are thrown back upon yourself, upon the Teacher within, upon Me, your own True Self.

Yes, all the deception, all the discipline, all the taking of your ardor and devotion — not to speak of your money and services — to what you believe to be My Work, and selfishly purloining and utilizing them for the upbuilding and strengthening of their own personal power and prestige among their followers; feeding each of you with just enough subtle flattery and promises of spiritual advancement, together with clever sophistry under the guise of high and beautiful sounding spiritual teaching, to keep you bound to them so you would continue to support and honor and glorify them, ever holding over you the lash of My displeasure if they receive not unquestioning trust and obedience, — yes, all this *I* permit to be, for it is what you desire and seek, and Desire is truly the agent of My Will.

You may be even giving to some other teacher, — either in the seen or the unseen and no matter how true, well-meaning and spiritually wise, — who you think cannot be classed with the kind just mentioned, your unquestioning love, devotion and obedience, and you may be receiving what you think are teachings and guidance of inestimable value.

All this is well, so long as you are receiving that which you seek and think you need; for I supply all things to satisfy such desires. But know that all such is vain and unproductive of the real results sought; for all seeking and all desire for spiritual attainment is of the personality and therefore selfish, and leads only to final disappointment, disillusionment and humiliation.

If you but can see it, it is in the disillusionment and humiliation that the real results are attainable, for those are what I opened up for you and led you towards, when presenting the possibility of getting help from some human teacher; and these, disillusionment and humiliation, and what I purposely brought you to, in order that, having become once more humble and docile as a little child, you would then be ready to listen to and obey My Word spoken within, and, hearing and obeying, you could enter into My Kingdom.

Yes, all outward seeking will end thus, and will but bring you back to Me, weary, naked, starving, willing to listen to My Teaching and to do anything for even a crust of My Bread, which in your stubbornness and conceit you disdained before and deemed not good enough for your proud Spirit.

Now, if you have had enough of teachings and teachers, and are sure that *within* you lies the Source of all Wisdom, these words will bring joy unspeakable to your heart. For do they not confirm that which you already have felt within to be true?

For you who cannot yet see this and still need a Mediator, I have provided the story of The Christ crucified for your redemption, picturing how I desire you to live that, through the crucifixion of your personality, you may rise in consciousness to Oneness with Me.

But to you who are strong enough to bear it, I say you need no mediator between you and Me, for we are One already. If you can but know it, you can come direct and *at once* to Me in consciousness. I, God within you will receive you and you shall abide with Me for ever and ever; even as does My Son Jesus, the Man of Nazareth, through Whom I AM even now expressing as I did express nineteen hundred years ago, and as I some day shall express through you.

To you who wonder how and why I say such beautiful and such spiritual things through personalities who fail to live up to the teachings they apparently of themselves give out, I say:

I use all avenues Impersonally to express My Meaning.

Some I have prepared to be better mediums of expression than others, but personally knowing nothing of Me.

In some I have quickened the heart the better to contain Me, thereby becoming consciously more at One with Me.

Some have become so at One with Me that they no longer are separated in consciousness from Me, and in Them I live and move and express My Spiritual Nature.

Since the earliest days of expression on earth I have prepared My Priests and My Prophets and My Messiahs to vision forth to the world My Idea — My Word that shall finally become flesh.

But whether I speak through Priest, Prophet or Messiah, or through a little child, or through your worst enemy, all words that appeal vitally to you are the words the I AM of *You* speaks through the organism of such medium to your Soul consciousness.

Should a number be gathered together to hear My Word spoken through one of My Priests, it is not the Priest of himself but *I, in the heart of each* hearer, Who draw from the Priest the vital words that sink deep into the consciousness of each. The Priest knows not what he says that so affects you, and may not even comprehend My Meaning of the words he speaks to you.

I within him do draw from the combined devotion to and belief in Me, consciously and unconsciously expressed by all those gathered around him, the Spiritual Force which serves as a channel or a connecting line through or over which I reach the consciousness of those minds I have prepared to comprehend My Meaning. For although I speak the same words to all, yet these words contain a distinct and separate message for each, and no one knows any but the message I speak to him; for I within you choose from the words the meaning I intend for you, and I within your brother and your sister likewise choose the meaning I intend for each of them.

When two or three are gathered together in My Name, there will I always be; for the Idea which draws them together I, within each, inspire — for it is My Idea. From the union of their aspirations towards Me do I create a medium or channel through which I enable the Soul consciousness to gain such glimpses of Me as each is capable of comprehending.

Every Priest, every Teacher, every Medium, I cause instinctively to know this, for they are My chosen Ministers; and I likewise cause to awaken in them a desire to surround themselves with followers, that I may quicken, in the hearts of those who are ready a consciousness of My Presence within. The Priest, the Teacher, or the Medium, themselves, may never have recognized Me within, and may be deeming Me as entitized or personalized in some master or guide or saviour *without* themselves; but nevertheless, there are those whom I lead to these, My Ministers, in whom, through certain words I cause My Ministers to speak, together with the Spiritual Force furnished by the various aspirants, I am enabled to awaken their Soul consciousness to a real comprehension of Me, the Impersonal One, seated within — in the very midst of All, in the heart of each.

For the I AM of My Minister, and the I AM of each follower are *One*, one in consciousness, one in understanding, one in love, and one in purpose, which purpose is the fulfillment of My Will.

This I AM, which is wholly Impersonal, and knows neither time, space nor different identities, merely utilizes the personalities of both Minister and followers, and the circumstance of personal contact, as a means of giving voice to My Idea, ever struggling within for outer expression.

Those Ministers who take the confidence and trust of My followers, and use it to further their own private purposes, I cause to awaken to a recognition of My Will and My Idea all in proper season. This awakening, however, is not pleasant to their personalities, and almost always causes much suffering and humiliation; but their souls rejoice and sing grateful praises to Me when I bring it to pass.

Therefore, wonder not at the sometimes wonderful words of Truth that come from mouths apparently unfit to speak them and comprehending not their meaning; nor at the fact that simple followers oftentimes awaken faster than and grow beyond their teachers. I Who dwell within both teacher and follower choose different conditions and provide different ways for the expression of My Attributes in each different Soul, fitting each into just the time and place where they can complement and help each other the best; thus uniting all into the most harmonious expression of My Idea possible under the circumstances.

XV. MASTERS

You, who are still holding to the idea, taught in various teachings, that I will provide a "Master" or Divine Teacher for each aspirant towards union with Me, hear My Words.

It is true I have permitted you in the past to delve into all kinds of mystical and occult books and teachings, encouraging your secret desire to acquire the powers necessary to attain this union extolled in such teachings, even to the extent of quickening in you some slight consciousness of the possession of such powers.

I have even permitted the belief that by practicing certain exercises, breathing in a certain way, and saying certain mantras, you might attract to you a "Master" from the unseen, who would become your teacher and help you to prepare for certain initiations that would admit you into an advanced Degree, in some secret Order in the inner planes of existence, where much of My Divine Wisdom would be opened up to you.

I have not only permitted these things, but, if you can see it, it was I who led you to these books, inspired in you such desire, and caused such belief to find lodgment in your mind; — but not for the purpose you imagine. Yes, I have brought you through all these teachings, desires and beliefs, trying to point out to your human mind the Forces I use to bring into expression My Divine Idea.

I have portrayed these Forces as heavenly Hierarchies, and that your human intellect might the better comprehend, I pictured them as Angels or Divine Beings, Impersonal agents or executors of My Will, engaged in the process of bringing into expression My Idea that was in the beginning. But you did not understand.

Your human intellect, enamored of the possibility of meeting and communing with one of these beings, as claimed in some of the teachings, proceeded at once to personalize Them, and began to long for

Their appearance in your life, imagining that They are interested in your *human* affairs, and that by living in accordance with certain rules set down in certain teachings, you could propitiate Them so They would help you to gain Nirvana or Immortality.

Now I have purposely permitted you to indulge yourself with such delusions, letting you long, and pray, and strive earnestly to obey all the instructions given; even leading you on, sometimes, by giving you glimpses, in self-induced visions and dreams, of ideal beings, which I permitted you to believe were such "Masters."

I may even have caused to open in you certain faculties, which make it possible for you to sense the presence of personalities that have passed into the spirit side of life, and who have been attracted by your desires and seek to fulfill the part of Master and Guide to you.

Now the time has come for you to know that such beings are *not* Masters, also that *Divine* Beings do not call themselves Masters; that I, and I alone, your own Real Self, AM the only Master for you now, and until you are able to know Me also in your brother; —

That any being, either in human or spirit form, that presents himself to your consciousness and claims to be a Master, or *who permits you to call him Master*, is nothing more nor less than a personality, the same as yours, and therefore is not Divine, as your human mind understands that term, despite the many wonderful "truths" he may utter, and the "marvelous" things he may do.

Just so long as your human mind seeks or worships the *idea* of a Master in any other being, no matter how lofty or sacred he may seem to you, just so long will you be fed with such ideas; until, verily, I may perhaps, permit you to meet and commune with such a "Master."

If that "privilege" *is* vouchsafed you, it will be only in order to hasten your awakening and your consequent disillusionment, when you will learn that "Master" is indeed but a *personality*, even though far more advanced in awakening than you, but still a personality — and not the Divine One your innermost Soul is yearning for you to know.

For I feed you with every idea that will operate to teach you the reality back of the seeming, and if I lead you on to apparent deception and loss of faith in all human teachings, and in all human and even Divine perfection, it is only to enable you the more clearly to distinguish between the substance and the shadow, and to prepare you for that far higher Ideal I am waiting to picture to you.

You can rise in your human personality only to the ideal your *human* mind is capable of conceiving. Through Desire I cause My Will to manifest in you, and through Desire I perform many wondrous works.

If you doubt this, you need only to apply the Key;

To think of a Master *is to create* one.

This idea of a Master, by your thinking, becomes what you desire and imagine a Master to be.

In other words, by your thinking you build around this idea, all the qualities you imagine a Master possesses. Your human mind, through Desire, through aspiration, through worship, must needs create these qualities in some *imaginary* being, who is still a personality, for you cannot as yet conceive of an *Impersonal* being.

Therefore, according to the intensity of your desire and thinking, must this idea sooner or later come into actual manifestation, either by attracting to you such a personality in the flesh, or one entitized in the realm of visions and dreams.

As your human mind is constituted, it at certain times thinks it needs a Master, one to whom it can turn with its human trials and problems for explanation and advice, thinking life's problems can be settled that way. If I draw to you one who fails you or deceives you and throws you back finally upon Me, your own Self, discouraged, disillusioned and humiliated, it is only that perhaps then you will be ready to turn to *Me within*, and will listen to *My* Voice, which all these years has been speaking to you, but to which your proud and egoistic mind has not deigned to listen.

You who have not yet had this experience, who have not yet met the Master of your aspirations, either in human or spirit form; you, within whom My Words have failed to awaken a quickening response to their truth, — for you I have in store certain experiences which will surely lead you to Me later on, and then you will be brought to know that I AM the Master, the *inspiring Idea* back of and within every thought of and every aspiration towards a Master that enters your mind, whether coming from within or without.

It is taught, "When the pupil is ready the Master appears." And this is true, in a sense; but not as you have interpreted it.

Your secret desire for a Master will bring him to you, but only when I have prepared you for such appearance. But such appearance will be only an *appearance* of a Master. The *true* Master or Teacher, when He appears, you may never recognize; for He may be hidden in an interesting friend, a business associate, your next door neighbor, or in your own wife or husband or child.

You, who have risen above Desire, you who no longer seek a Master or a Teacher, or even Me, but are abiding alone in the faith of My Eternal Presence and Promise, — for you I have in store a meeting and a communion, which will bring to your Soul such joy and blessings as your human mind is incapable of conceiving.

Now, this is a mystery, and until you can comprehend it, you are justified in claiming the above as not consistent with certain statements herein, and as contradicting teachings in My other Revelations.

Fear not; this mystery will be revealed unto you – if you truly wish to know My Meaning.

Until then, why, in your seeking, be satisfied with anything short of the Highest?

Why seek in human or spirit teacher, guide, master or angel, for the necessarily *limited* manifestation of My Perfection, when you can come *directly* to Me, God within you, the Omniscient, Omnipotent, Omnipresent, the Inspiring Idea back of and within *All* manifestations?

As I AM in You, even as I AM in any you seek, and as all the Wisdom, all the Power and all the Love they possess come only from Me, why not now come to *Me*, and let *Me* prepare you also so I can express My All through *You*?

You are a human personality, yet You are Divine and therefore Perfect.

The first of these truths you believe, the latter you do not believe.

Yet *both* are true. — *That* is the mystery.

You *are* just what you *think* You are.

One or the other, *which* are you? — Or both?

You are *One with Me*. I AM in You, in Your human personality, in Your body, mind and intellect. I AM in every cell of Your body, in every attribute of Your mind, in every faculty of Your intellect. I AM the Soul, the active Principle of each. You are in Me. You are a Cell of my Body; You are an Attribute of My Mind; You are a Faculty of My Intellect. You are a part of Me, yet You are I, My Self. We are One, and always have been.

This idea of a Master I brought to your mind's attention was only to lead you to and prepare you for this Idea of Me, your Impersonal Self, an Angel of Light, a Radiation of My Being, your own Divine Lord and Master, *within*.

Yes, *I*, your Divine Self, AM the Master your Soul has caused you to seek, and when you do find Me, and *know* I AM your Self, then will you in your human consciousness gladly become My Disciple, will lovingly wait upon Me, and will be concerned only that you faithfully serve Me, both within yourself and within your fellow men. And then will you understand why only "One is your Master, even Christ."

For I as the Christ dwell in all men and AM their One and Only Self. Through all men I AM ever calling to you and trying to reach and impress your human consciousness. As I AM continually teaching you, not only through all men but through every avenue needed at the time, I have many ways of reaching your consciousness and utilize all to bring you to a realization of My Meaning.

I speak with many voices, — with the voice of all human emotions, passions and desires. I speak with Nature's voice, with the voice of Experience, even with the voice of *human* knowledge.

Yes, these are all My Voice, which I use Impersonally to express to you the *one fact*, that I AM in All and that I AM All. What this Voice says, in Its thousand ways, is that you, too, are part of this All, and that I AM in *you*, waiting for your recognition of Me and your *conscious* cooperation in the expression of My Idea of Impersonal Perfection on earth, even as It is expressing in Heaven.

When this recognition comes, and then only, are you ready to meet and know a *real* Master. Then and then only will you realize why I, your own Impersonal Self can be and AM the only possible Master of your human personality.

Then also will you understand why in your personal, separate consciousness you could never recognize or know a real Master should you meet Him in a physical body, — that not until you are able to enter into your Christ Consciousness, My Consciousness within you and within Him, He would not exist to you other than perhaps as a kind and helpful friend or teacher.

When you have attained to that Consciousness, then only will you be worthy and qualified to know and commune with your fellows in the Great Brotherhood of the Spirit, Those who have mastered self and Who live only to help Their younger brothers also to find the Divine One within.

If a being should come into your life who seemed to you Divine and who let you think or call him a Master, he is not yet wholly Impersonal. Such a one might be a master-man, but he would not be the Divine One your Soul yearns to serve.

Perhaps you would be satisfied to have such a one for a Master, even if he were not wholly Impersonal. If so, then I would hereafter bring you to a realization of *his* personal imperfections by a constant comparison with *My* Impersonal Perfection; until you would finally turn and come to Me in complete abandon, acknowledging Me and My Impersonality as the only Model and Ideal, and as the true Cause which inspired your long search without for My Perfection, that could be found only within, hidden deep within your own Soul.

XVI. THE CHRIST AND LOVE

To you who fear that My Words may destroy your belief in and love for the Lord Jesus Christ, I say:

Nearly two thousand years ago, when the process of the expression of My Idea had reached the stage where I could show forth some of My Divine *Reality*, in order to do this and to recall to My human Attributes their mission on earth, it became necessary to express through a human personality and to manifest in a human form My *Divine* Attributes, so their human minds and intellects could see and remember and be inspired by Me within to let My Idea similarly express through and manifest in their human personalities.

This I did through the personality of Jesus, the man of Galilee, picturing to the human understanding by My Teachings given through Him, and by My *Life* manifested by Him, what was necessary in order to express fully My Divine Idea.

I showed, by the experiences of a symbolic nature through which I caused His human personality I created for such purpose to pass, what all personalities must pass through before you, My human Attributes, who created these personalities, can again become Impersonal enough to be conscious expressors with Me of My Divine Idea.

All of you, My human Attributes, before the I AM within can awaken your human minds to a realization of Me, your Divine Self must be born of a Virgin Love in a humble manger — the place where the cattle come to feed (the humble and contrite heart filled with faith and trust in God, to which state the human or animal nature must come). You must then be taken into Egypt, the land of darkness (or intellectual activity), there to grow and thrive in body and understanding until you become strong with the feeling of Me within. Then, when you are sufficiently conscious of *My* Power and *My* Love, will I begin to speak through you words of Wisdom and Truth, which will confound the learned of the world, even the Doctors of the Law. Then will follow a long period of study and meditation, which ripens the mind and develops the Soul, until you arrive at full maturity of the I AM Consciousness within, and which prepare you for your baptism in the Jordan, when you will be opened completely to Me, to the full consciousness that You and I are One, that there is no separation, that I AM your Real Self; and I AM henceforth permitted wholly to direct your lives.

I then *lead* you out into the world, called in My other Revelation the Wilderness, there to try you and make you strong and to accustom you to the Impersonal use of My Divine Attributes I bring to you three great Temptations of Power, Self-Righteousness, and Money, until you have proven that nothing of the intellect, nothing of the self, nothing from without, can tempt you to forget Me within, and that My Voice and Mine alone, whether speaking in your heart or in the hearts of your brothers, is the only Voice you are now capable of hearing.

This proven, there will begin the period of performing miracles and of teaching the multitude, accompanied by the revilement and persecution of the unbelieving and scoffing world; followed by the trial before Pontius Pilate, the representative of the Worldly Law; the sentence; the ascent of Calvary carrying the Cross; the being nailed upon the Cross; the Agony; the three days in the tomb; and then the final resurrection, when you enter into complete union with Me.

All of which has its inner meaning, or Soul application, and which should be readily understood by you, if you have opened your heart to Me.

Such has been The Way in the past for you and for all who have studied and followed My Teachings, given forth in My former Revelations. Now the time has come when I have prepared you and many for a new Dispensation, wherein you can enter into the consciousness of Me direct and *at once* by the Impersonal Way. Those who are big enough and strong enough to throw off all claims of the human personality, and who can say I AM, and *know I AM The ONE within* Who gives them this strength and enables them to rise above the attractions and influences of the outer world, — those are the ones I have chosen through whom to express all the wondrous glories of My Divine Idea.

The Christ, or the I AM Consciousness, must be born in your heart and in the heart of every human personality, must grow and thrive and pass through in some manner every experience symbolized in the life of Jesus, before you can come to this point and become a conscious expressor with Me of My Divine Idea. The example of the Christ Love and Compassion which I expressed in that Life must you also express in some degree in your life, before you can taste of the fruits of that Love, which in reality is not love, but the Holy Three-in-One, — Love-Wisdom-Power, that is the true expression of My *Impersonal* Life.

You heretofore have not known the meaning of the Impersonal Life, hence you could not know the meaning of Impersonal Love. Love to you, if you will carefully analyze that feeling, has always been a human emotion or expression; and you have been unable to conceive of a love devoid of or unattached to some human or personal interest. Now, as you begin to feel *Me* within your heart and open it wide to contain Me, will I fill you with a wondrous strange new feeling, which will quicken every fibre of your being with the creative instinct, and be to you a veritable Elixir of Life. For in the outer expression of *that* feeling, when I thus, through you, pour it forth into the world, will you taste of the unutterable sweetness of My Holy *Impersonal* Love, with Its accompanying illumination of mind and consciousness of unlimited Power; and It will make you a wholly selfless and therefore perfect channel for the Impersonal expression of My Divine Idea.

You will then realize that you are part of Me and part of every other being, and that all you have or are, is not yours, but Mine, for Use wherever and however I direct.

Your life will no longer be centered in your self, but that self will be lost, merged in your other Selves, giving freely of your Life, your Understanding, your Strength, your Substance, which are but phases of

My Impersonal Life or My Impersonal Love, that I have portioned out to you only for such use.

In the personality of Jesus, the Christ, I manifested much of the Love Impersonal, enough to inspire and lead you into seeking to emulate His Life and His Personality, and, through such seeking and striving, to awaken in you the Consciousness of the Christ within *you*. Through this awakening and the realization that the Christ is but the channel or door that opens unto Me, I have finally brought you to the point where you can enter in and consciously become a part of My Impersonal Life.

I here tell you plainly that My Impersonal Love has naught to do with personal lives and personal loves. All such are but the outer mediums I use through which to pour from out the heart of Humanity into the world My Real Love, where it is ever expressing its all-embracing, vitalizing, creative, and uplifting Power.

My Love considers not individuals or personalities; they are but pawns on the chess-board of life which I move as I deem best to accomplish My purpose, — the full and complete expression in Humanity of My Divine Idea.

In Humanity only can I express My Idea, even as you can express your idea of yourself only in and through your human personality.

In Humanity I live and move and have My Being. It is the mortal personality and body of My Immortal Self, even as your personality and its body is what you use to express your being.

All individual human personalities with their bodies are but the cells of My Body of Humanity. Just as the I AM of you is now building your body so that through it You can perfectly express My Idea of you, or your Real Self, so am I gradually building Humanity so that through It I can perfectly express My Idea of My Self.

As the individual cells of My Body of Humanity, even as those of your human body, by partaking of My Life, become Impersonal and harmonious parts of the organs they form, they live a healthy and happy life. But let one cell oppose or act contrary to the general law of its organ, and the harmonious functioning of that organ becomes impossible, which naturally affects the whole body and results in disease.

Every cell of an organ is an integral part of that organ, and its work is necessary to that organ's perfect functioning and to the perfect health of My Body. So that unless each cell gives up *all* its power and *all* its intelligence, which are but attributes of the Life I give it, toward the perfect functioning of My entire Body, the only result for My Body can be inharmony, with its consequent effects, — disease, suffering, sin, bondage, poverty, lack of understanding, disintegration, or death.

Likewise, unless each organ gives up all the intelligence and all the powers with which I endowed it, to the one purpose of expressing and maintaining the life of My Body in perfect health, the only result can be disorganization, disruption, rebellion, and finally WAR, — war between the various organs and between their respective cells, and a greater or lesser consequent chaotic condition in My whole Body.

In My Body of Humanity this would mean war between Nations, which are the Organs of My Body. As all war is but acute disease or disharmony, and as My Life, which in Humanity manifests as Impersonal Love, can express only in harmony —even as in the physical body, It is always utilizing, equalizing and preparing conditions so that It can thus express.

This It does either by eradicating gradually from the various organs of the body all disease, weakened and unfit cells, or by developing the disease into a malignant form — such as fever, dropsy, carbuncles, blood-poisoning, or degeneracy, in the physical body. It throws off such cells quickly by the billions, until a particular organ either is purified or its power of functioning is wholly destroyed.

In other words, the real life and work of each cell and of each organ lies in giving up its individual life that My whole Body can Be or Express in perfect harmony. When each cell and each organ has no other idea than this, and makes itself a pure and selfless channel through which My Impersonal Life can flow, then has My Body become a harmonious and perfect Whole; and then can My Idea express on earth Its Divine powers and possibilities, even as it does in the Celestial Realm of the Eternal.

As you give up your self wholly to Me that I can pour through you My Holy, Impersonal Love, having no other thought than the perfect expression of that Love, which is My Real Life, then will I through you be enabled to quicken and awaken those about you gradually to a recognition of Me, The Christ within *them*, so that they too will likewise give up their selves wholly to Me. Finally the organ, or that particular part of My Body of Humanity you and they form, attains perfect health and harmony, and adds its quota to the bringing about and maintaining of perfect health in My entire Body.

When such time comes, My Divine Life Force, or My Impersonal Love, will be flowing and manifesting throughout all Humanity, and My Idea will be expressing fully on earth even as It is in Heaven. The earth and all earthly bodies will no longer be of the gross physical material they formerly seemed, but they will have become utterly purified and cleansed of the self, and will have been again lifted up to whence they descended. For the purpose of their creation, that of developing organisms for the outward manifestation and human expression of My Divine Idea, will have been accomplished; and having no further use for physical or outward mediums of such expression, I hereafter will create and express only with Mind Substance, which is the only medium needed in the Heavenly World of the Impersonal Life.

XVII. FINDING ME

You, who have studied carefully all that has been said herein, and who think you have gotten a glimpse of Me, but yet are not sure, come close, and listen with your Soul to what I now have to say.

Be still! — and KNOW, — I AM, — GOD.

If you have learned to "Be Still," if you have studied and meditated upon this "I" as God within you, if you are able to distinguish It from the personal I, and are conscious at times of being able to step outside, as it were, of your personality and view your human self as it is, see all its petty faults and weaknesses, its base selfishness, its animal appetites and passions, its childish desires and foolish pride and vanities;

If you can do all this and have seen these things with clear vision, know that at those moments you have been One with Me in consciousness, that it was your Real Self, I within you, permitting you thus to see with My Eyes the Reality of things.

At those moments you were freed from your personality and were dwelling in My Consciousness, call it Cosmic, Universal, Spiritual or Impersonal Consciousness, as you will; for you could not have seen these things in your self except through Impersonal eyes, My Eyes.

Again, if you will look back you will recall many times when you felt strongly impelled to do certain things, some of which you did, with perfect results; others of which you argued against, your intellect reasoning you into different action, and often with failure, disappointment or suffering as a result.

This impelling consciousness was only your Real Self, I within you, at such moments guiding you, distinctly telling you what to do. At those moments you were hearing with your Spiritual ears, My Ears, and when you Impersonally obeyed, success and satisfaction followed, but when you personally thought you knew better, discomfiture, regret and unhappiness resulted.

Again, there have been moments when you have *felt* approaching events, or the nearness of unseen persons, or inharmonious vibrations when contacting others.

This is only the *real* You feeling with your Spiritual or Impersonal Body, whose consciousness, did you but know it, is ever on the alert to protect and warn and advise you regarding all outer things, conditions and events.

The best and surest way you may know Me is when Selfless Love fills your heart, and there is a strong, compelling urge to help some one, to heal their ills, to relieve their suffering, to bring them happiness, to point out the True Way, — that is the actual feel of Me within you, pushing the personality aside, using your mind and body for the purpose I created them, as avenues for the expression of My Real Nature, which is Perfect Love, the Christ of God, the one, vitalizing, quickening, life-giving, strengthening, healing, all-supplying, all-informing Power in the Universe.

All this is pointed out to you in order to impress upon you that it is I, in your Spiritual body, the Perfect Body within, where I dwell, Who am always thus talking to you, advising you, teaching you, warning and helping you, in all the affairs of life, yes, in every little detail.

If you will but turn to Me, and will carefully watch for and study these impressions which you are receiving every moment, and will learn to trust them, and thus to wait upon and rest in *Me*, putting all your faith in Me, verily I will guide you in all your ways; I will solve for you all your problems, make easy all your work, and you will be led among green pastures, beside the still waters of life.

Ah, My child, if you will spend but one-tenth of the time and energy you have wasted in seeking without among the husks of human knowledge and human teachings, in earnest, determined efforts directed within to find Me;

If you will devote but one hour each day thus to Me alone, imagining and practicing the Presence of Me within you;

I here promise you that you will not only soon, very soon find Me, but I will be to you an exhaustless fount of such Wisdom and Strength and Help, as your human mind now cannot possibly conceive.

Yes, if you will but seek Me thus, making Me FIRST in your life, never resting until you do find Me, it will not be long before you will become conscious of My Presence, of My Loving Voice, speaking constantly from out of the depths of your heart.

You will learn to come to Me in Sweet Communion, and you will find yourself abiding in My consciousness, and that My Word is abiding in you, and that whatever you desire will in seemingly miraculous ways be done unto you.

This abiding *continually* in Me may be difficult at first, for the World, the Flesh and the Devil are still presenting evidence to your consciousness. But you will become accustomed to the use of My Impersonal Eyes, and will soon be able to see into the Reality of things, even into the Reality of these seeming Lords of the Earth. Then you will find you are dwelling in a wondrous *new* World, peopled with Angelic Beings, using the Flesh bodies of Their human personalities merely as vehicles, or instruments, or clothing, in which to contact the earthly conditions and experiences They have created, in order to develop the Soul qualities necessary for the perfect expression on earth of *My Idea*.

To your eyes then there will be no shadows, no evil, and consequently no Devil; for all is Light and Love, Freedom, Happiness and Peace, and you will see *Me in all*, in each Being some attribute of Me, in each animate thing some phase of Me; and you will need only to let My Love shine from out your heart and It will illumine for you the Real meaning of *all* that you see.

Then the great Realization will come that you have found the Kingdom of God, that you are walking in It, that It is right here on this earth, that It is manifesting all around you, that you have been living in It all the time, but you did not know it;

That instead of being without in some far off place, It is within your own being, within every other being, the innermost inner of all manifested things.

In other words, It will be found to be the REALITY of ALL things, and that all outward seeming is but the shadow of this Reality, created by man's misconceptions and his belief in his separateness from Me.

When you have found The Kingdom, you will likewise find your place in It, realizing now that you are in truth one of My Divine Attributes, that your work was all laid out for you from the beginning, and that all that has gone before has been but a preparation and a fitting of your human personality for that work.

Your whole Soul will leap with joyful anticipation, that, after all these many years of wandering, you have at last returned to My Home, and can now enter into My Real Life, One in Consciousness with Me and with your other Selves, all working to bring about the final perfect expression on earth of My Divine Idea.

You, to whom the reading of this has brought memories of previous joys and whose Soul has quickened in response, do not leave these words until you have gotten from them all I have to tell you. Be Still! and listen to My inner Voice, and learn of the glories that await — if you are able to see with Impersonal Eyes and hear with Impersonal Understanding.

However, if this reading brings to you your first vision of My Reality within you, setting in motion, by this partial realization of Me and My Kingdom, high vibrations which lift you into a temporary Spiritual ecstasy, and you resolve to try to abide always in this Consciousness of Me, and always to obey Me, — do not be discouraged should you fail when immediately thereafter an occasion comes to test the sincerity and strength of your resolve.

It is only by your trying and failing and realizing keenly your lack of strength and ability to rest and trust in Me, that I can quicken in you the consciousness of My Divine Powers ever waiting to manifest through you.

These high vibrations are only the arousing into action of certain *Soul* qualities and their corresponding faculties, which must be awakened before I can manifest such Powers.

And naturally when such Soul qualities are aroused, they meet active opposition from certain other qualities which heretofore held undisputed sway in your nature, and which must be overcome and brought under subjection and then lifted up into their true service before the Soul qualities can freely express.

And this opposition should and will strengthen and test and perfect the expression of these Soul qualities, for you must be capable of withstanding every attack from without before you can fully manifest all My Divine Powers pushing forth from within.

Know that I am manifesting these Powers in you just as fast as you can bear it and be strong.

The mistake you make is in trying to grow yourself.

I AM the Tree of Life within you. My Life will and must push forth, but It will do it by gradual and steady growth. You cannot come into your fruitage before you have grown to it. Remember, My Life is all the time building you up into the perfection of health and strength and beauty, that must express outwardly as It is even now expressing within.

You who have begun to realize I AM within, but have not yet learned to commune with Me, listen and learn now.

You have learned to "Be Still," and you have perhaps *felt* My Presence within. If so, realizing *I AM* there, ask Me a question. Then, with a silent, earnest prayer to Me for an answer, but without anxiety, care or personal interest, and with an open mind, wait confidently for the impressions that will come.

Should a thought come in answer that you recognize as what you have heard or read somewhere, cast it out immediately, and say, "No. Father, what do *you* say?"

Other thoughts may come from other human sources, but if you are alert you will recognize them as such and refuse to accept them. Then if you *persist* in asking *Me*, *you* will finally get an answer that you will *feel* is really from Me.

Thus it will be at *first*. When you have learned to distinguish *My* Voice from all other voices, and can keep your personal interest wholly suppressed, then will you be able to hold silent communion with Me at will, without interference from others' ideas, beliefs, and opinions; and you can ask any question you wish, or another can ask you any question on any problem on which they need help, and *I will that moment place in your mind the words to speak*, either silently to yourself, or audibly through your tongue to the other.

You, My Beloved, who have consecrated your self to Me, and are bending every effort to find union with Me, but instead have found apparently that every prop of the World's support has been withdrawn or is being withdrawn, and that you are without money and without friends and know not where to turn for human help;

Learn, My Blessed One, that you are very, very close now, and that if you will only continue to abide in Me, letting My Word abide in and guide you, resting and trusting absolutely in My Promise, I will very soon bring to you a Joy, a Fulfillment, a Peace, that human words and human minds can not possibly picture.

For you have obeyed My Commands, and you have *trusted* Me, and have sought first My Kingdom and My Righteousness, and therefore will I add all other things unto you, even those the World has denied you.

You, My Dear One, who likewise have consecrated your self to Me, but who are still holding to some of the World's standards, being unable to let go and trust wholly to Me;

You to whom, therefore, I have permitted failure, disappointment, even poverty, in order to let you learn the false value of all worldly things, their impermanence, their lack of power to provide happiness, their having nothing to do with My Real Life;

You, dear child, who do not yet see this and whose heart is full of anxiety and fear because you do not see where tomorrow's bread is coming from, or the money for next week's rent, or for the past due mortgage;

Listen once more to My Words long since given to you in the Sermon on the Mount.

"Therefore I say unto you, Take no thought for your life, what ye shall eat or what ye shall drink; nor yet for your body, what ye shall put on.

"Is not the life more than meat, and the body than raiment?

"Behold the fowls of the air; for they sow not, neither do they reap, nor gather into barns; yet your heavenly Father feedeth them. Are ye not much better than they?

"Which of you by taking thought can add one cubit unto his stature?

"And why take ye thought for raiment? Consider the lilies of the field, how they grow; they toil not neither do they spin; and yet I say unto you that even Solomon in all his glory was not arrayed like one of these.

"Wherefore, if God so clothe the grass of the field, which today is and tomorrow is cast into the oven, shall he not much more clothe you, O ye of little faith?

"Therefore take no thought, saying, What shall we eat? or What shall we drink? or Wherewithal shall we be clothed?

"(For after all these things do the Gentiles seek.) For your heavenly Father knoweth that ye have need of these things.

"But seek ye first the kingdom of God (being interpreted His Consciousness) and His righteousness; and all these things shall be added unto you.

"Take, therefore, no thought for the morrow, for the morrow shall take thought for the things of itself.

"Sufficient unto the day is the evil thereof."

Do you need any more definite Commands or any more definite Promise than these? — You who have consecrated yourself to Me, and call yourself My disciple.

Listen!

Have I not always provided everything? Have you ever been in need but what I always appeared with help just at the right moment? Has there ever been a time when things looked dark that I did not bring Light?

Can you, with what you know now, look back over your life and see where you could have ordered it better? Would you exchange your *Spiritual* understanding for the earthly possessions of any one you know? Have I not done all this, despite the fact you have been rebelling and refusing to listen to Me all your life?

Ah, My Children, can you not see that money, home, clothes, food, and their acquirement are only incidents and have nothing to do with your *real* Life, excepting as you make them real by thinking into them so much importance, and letting Me remain only a side issue?

If it becomes necessary for you to be deprived of the things of the world that you may learn the Truth, — that I AM the *only* important thing in Life, that I *must* be *FIRST* if you *truly* love Me, — I permit this that *real* and *lasting* Happiness and Prosperity can be yours.

This applies to you also, My Child, you who have lost health, have lost courage, have lost all hold of your Self, and after weary years of seeking without from earthly physicians and remedies, following faithfully every instruction and suggestion given, in order to regain the Life you have lost, — you who have turned finally within to Me, with the faint hope that I may be able to help you.

Know, My Little One, that you, too, must come in complete surrender to Me, the One and Only Physician who can heal you. For I AM the Life Omnipotent within you. I AM your Health, your Strength, your Vitality. Not until you can *feel ME* within, and know I AM all this to you, is real and lasting Health for you to experience.

And now, My Child, draw close. For I AM now going to tell you the means of obtaining all these things — Health, Prosperity, Happiness, Union, Peace.

In the following words lies hidden the Great Secret. Blessed be you who find it.

Be still! And KNOW, — *I AM*, — GOD.

KNOW I AM *in you*. KNOW I AM *you*. KNOW I AM your *LIFE*. KNOW *All* Wisdom, *All* Love, *All* Power abides in this Life, which is flowing freely through your entire being *NOW*.

I AM the LIFE, *I AM* the INTELLIGENCE, *I AM* the POWER in *all* Substance, — in all the cells of your body; in the cells of all mineral, vegetable and animal matter; in fire, water and air; in Sun, Moon and Stars. I AM that in you and in them which IS. Their consciousness is One with your consciousness, and All is My Consciousness. Through My Consciousness in them All that they have or are is yours — for the asking.

Speak to them then IN MY NAME.

Speak in the Consciousness of your Oneness with Me.

Speak in the Consciousness of My Power in you and of My Intelligence in them.

Speak – COMMAND what You WILL in this Consciousness, — and the Universe will rush to obey.

RISE UP! O aspirant for union with Me. Accept now your Divine Heritage! Open wide your Soul, your mind, your body, and breathe in My Breath of Life!

KNOW that I AM filling you full to overflowing with My Divine POWER, that every fibre, every nerve, every cell, every atom of your being is *now consciously ALIVE* with Me, alive with *My* Health, with *My* Strength, with *My* Intelligence with *My* BE-ING!

For I AM *within* you. We are not separated. We could not possibly be separated. For I AM *You*. I AM your *REAL* Self, your *REAL Life* and I AM manifesting My SELF and *ALL MY POWERS* in you *NOW*.

AWAKE! Rise up and assert your Sovereignty! *KNOW* your SELF and your POWERS! KNOW that *all I have* is yours, that My Omnipotent LIFE is flowing through you, that you can take of IT and build with IT what you WILL, and IT will manifest for you as Health, Power, Prosperity, Union, Happiness, Peace, — anything you WILL of ME.

Imagine this. THINK it. *KNOW* it! Then, with all the *Positiveness* of your nature, *Speak* the *Creative WORD!* It will not return to you void.

But know, Beloved, that this cannot be until you have come to Me in complete and utter surrender, until you have given yourself, your substance, your affairs, your Life into My keeping, putting all care and responsibility upon Me, resting and trusting in Me absolutely.

When you have done this, then will the above Words quicken into active life My Divine Powers latent in your Soul, and you will be conscious of a Mighty FORCE within you, which, just to the extent that you abide in Me, and let My Words abide in you, will free you entirely from your Dream World, will quicken you fully in Spirit, will make all the way clear for you, supply all things you desire, and lift trouble and suffering from you forevermore. Then will there be no more doubts and questionings, for you will KNOW that I, God your very Self, will always provide, will always point out the way; for You will have found that *You and I are One.*

XVIII. UNION

You, who truly wish to consecrate yourself thus to Me, and are willing to give your *whole* Life to Me, putting aside all personal ideas, hopes and aims, in order that I may freely and fully express through you My Impersonal Idea, listen carefully to these Words.

I have led you through all your experiences of life up to just this point. If you are now really ready and willing to serve Me, and have learned that you, of yourself, can know nothing and can do nothing, and that I AM, and what you call *your* intelligence and *your* strength and *your* substance are really Mine, and that it is I who direct all your thoughts and both cause and enable you to do all that you do, — then can you comprehend the significance of My Words, and are quite prepared to obey them.

I have hitherto brought to you the experiences that would teach you just these things. But now, if you are ready and worthy, you shall work *consciously* with Me, joyfully yet calmly awaiting each new experience, knowing that in each are contained marvelous expressions of My Meaning, which I will make altogether clear to you, and which will more and more bring you into loving, intimate union with Me.

Thus all experiences will hereafter be blessings, instead of trials and tests, or karmic effects of previous acts; for in each will I disclose unto you glorious visions of My Reality — of your own True, Wonderful Self; until you no longer will have any disposition to follow any of the old desires but will seek only to know *My* wishes and to please *Me*.

This will manifest in many new ways. In your activities, be they what they may, you will care not what the task, but do whatever lies before you, knowing that is what I require; and striving always and only to please Me by your *Impersonal* part in the doing, which enables Me thus *speedily* to accomplish My Will.

In your business even, you will find I AM there. In fact, it is I Who provide you with such business, *whatever* it be; not that in it you can be the success or the failure or the common plodder you are, nor that you can pile up riches for your descendants, or lose all that you have, or never accumulate any. No, but that through the success or failure, or lack of ambition or special ability, I may quicken your heart to a realization of Me, The Impersonal One, seated within; inspiring and directing all these things that you do, waiting for you consciously to participate in the *true* Success and accept of the *real* Riches I have in store for you.

You will then learn that your business, or labor, or condition of life, are but incidents, or the outer vehicles I choose and use to carry you through certain experiences which I deem best adapted to bring you to this realization; and at the same time to quicken in you certain Soul qualities that now but imperfectly express.

If you can but *know* Me, dwelling thus in your heart, accompanying you to your office, to your shop, to your labor, whatever it be, and will permit Me to direct your business and all your ways; verily I say unto you, when you can do this, you will at once become conscious of a new Power within you, a Power that will flow forth from you as a gentle, kindly sympathy, a true brotherliness, a loving helpfulness to all with whom you come in contact, inspiring them to higher principles of business and of life, creating in them a longing to shed a similar influence within their own circle; a Power that will attract to you business, money, friends, and abundance of all things you *need*; a Power that will connect you with the highest realms of thought, enabling you both to vision clearly and to manifest consciously all My Impersonal Powers and Attributes every moment of your life.

You will no longer feel any need to go to church or to religious meetings of any kind, or even to read the teachings of My Revelations, in order to find Me and to worship Me.

Instead you will turn *within* and always find Me *there*, and you will be so filled with the joy of communing with and serving Me, and of *thus* worshipping Me, that you will care not for any other thing than just to listen to and obey My Voice, and to feel the warmth and thrill of My Tender Love, as It fills and surrounds you and prepares the way and softens the conditions wherever you go and whatever be your work.

You I will cause to be an uplifting and leavening influence in the community wherever I send you, drawing all men to Me to receive My Blessing through you, who now are able so to make your personality subservient to My Holy Impersonality that they forget you and see only Me, and feel the quickening of My Presence within their own hearts; so that they go forth with a new light in their eyes and the sense of a new purpose in their lives.

In your homes particularly will I dwell. Through those nearest you will I teach you many wonderful things, which now you can understand, when before you passionately rebelled against their truth. Through husband, wife, child, brother, sister, parent, will I now be able to develop in you these great qualities, — patience, gentleness, forebearance, tongue-control, loving-kindness, true unselfishness, and an understanding heart; for I will cause you to see that I AM deep down in *their* hearts as I AM in yours.

Now will you be able to appreciate this and profit by it. When you truly do comprehend this great truth you will be able to see *Me* in your brother or your wife or your parent or child, appealing to you with loving, joyful eyes, when they speak. Instead of blaming them for their seeming mistakes, you will turn *within* to Me, the Impersonal One, Who will speak through you gentle words of loving kindness, which will immediately soften the heart of the other, and bring you once more together, and closer than ever before. For I, the *real I*, in the heart of each, am One, *and always respond when thus called upon.*

Yes, if you can but know it, your greatest school and your greatest teacher is in your own home, by your own fireside. Much, very much is reserved for those who consciously know this and permit Me, the Impersonal One within, to do the teaching. For I will not only teach you many things through the mouths of those nearest you, but I will teach those others similarly through you, — but with this difference: if *you are conscious* of Me and Impersonally are resting in Me and My Wisdom, then *you* will permit *Me* to inspire your words and to empower your acts, and you will not be concerned about their effects upon others or upon yourself, putting all responsibility upon Me.

When you can do this, you will marvel at the changes you see taking place, both in your personality and in the personalities of your dear ones — until you are able to see, back of their human personalities, Me, your own Impersonal Self, shining from out their eyes.

When you *can* thus see Me, then will the heavens be opened unto you, and no more will you see flaws in your brother, or hear inharmony around you, or feel unkindness coming from any other fellow being. For you will *know* that I, the Impersonal One, within that other, AM the fount of all perfection, of all harmony, of all loving-kindness, and wait but for the human personality to make the recognition, step submissively aside, and let My Light shine forth, resplendent in all the glory of My Divine Idea.

Then will you see that all conditions in which I put you are the places I have chosen where you can best serve Me; that in all places and in all conditions there is much, very much to do. The more objectionable they are to the personality, the more need there is of My Living Presence.

Wherever you are when the awakening comes, whatever has been your training, — in business, in a profession, in manual labor, in the church, or in the underworld, — there lies perhaps your best opportunity to serve; for there you know best the manner and the way. For how can My and Your other selves awaken to a knowledge of My Presence within, without the quickening influence which must first come from without. You who have received must give. You who have been quickened must become the quickener. You must take into this business, into this profession, into this labor, into this underworld, My Living Presence, must open the doors of the saddened and sickened heart and let My Light and My Healing Love pour in. You must supply the leaven that will leaven the lump. If these conditions are to be lifted up, you, My awakened one, must carry to these, My ignorant and betrayed ones, My Inspiration, My Blessing, My Strength, that they can rise up and throw off the influence of the world's ways, can harken to My Voice within, and can hereafter be the master of surrounding conditions and no longer the slave. No condition in life can be lifted up or conquered by running away from it. The Divine touch is needed and must be supplied. It can only be supplied by one who has sounded the depths as well as reached the heights of human experience, with *Me* as Guide and Interpreter.

You who read, and whose Soul comprehends, are blessed, and your work lies before you.

But you who still hesitate while your personality quakes in fear as the Light filters through your clouded intellect, — you, too, will soon partake of My Blessings; for I am rapidly preparing you for the joy that awaits.

Both you who comprehend and you who fear, know that I AM even now manifesting My Will through you; and the time will surely come when you will know no other Will but Mine, and when all things *You* Will, will come to pass and you will awaken fully from your Dream of Separation, and know Me as your Real and Only Self.

This will not be until you have given yourself and everything in your life wholly over to Me, and there is nothing left in *your* human personality to attract from others the slightest inharmonious thought or feeling, by act or word of yours.

Your way *then* will be one continuous round of blessing. Wherever you go will My Light shine and My Love radiate forth about you, creating Peace, Concord, Unity. The great thing will be, though not great but natural when once you understand, that every one will be better and happier by reason of your appearance in their lives.

For the I AM in them, while still in the flesh, has found or sensed within *you* a truly Impersonal avenue of expression, and therefore feels, though not consciously by the personality, the Glory and the Holiness of My Impersonal Life.

THE END.

BOOK TWO
THE WAY OUT

"The Way Out" was originally published with "The Way Beyond".

We know that with many finances are often a problem. All followers of Jesus Christ should learn the law which if obeyed will enable them to rise out of all conditions of lack, limitation, inharmony, disease and unhappiness that may manifest. You ask if this is really possible, and if there is a law which if obeyed will enable us to accomplish all that.

We say emphatically, there is such a law, and that you can be free from the fear and dominance of money, that you can have an abundance of all good things, that you can be well and happy, and can bring about an adjustment into perfect harmony to all departments of your life if you want these things enough to train yourself to obey this law. You say that you would do anything to obtain such wonderful blessings, if it is humanly possible.

It is not only possible, but everyone who is filled with such a desire can do it. For know a great truth, that you are permitted to be in such unhappy conditions by your Higher Self solely in order that you may seek and gain the knowledge, the power and the ability to control them, in order to free yourself forever from them and to assume your true place in life, and therein receive the heritage of good that is here for you, whenever you become wise and strong enough to claim it and use it for the good of others and not for selfish ends.

First know that it is all a matter of consciousness, and that you, yourself alone, are to blame for these conditions: for you alone created them and are firmly holding them in your consciousness or they would not be so plainly manifesting. All this we are taught in those great words, "As a man thinketh in his heart, so is he".

We know that you have heard this stated perhaps many times before, and so often that it may have become an old story. Some of you have tried to prove it and to rid your consciousness of all your negative thoughts; but because it took determined and persistent effort you soon grew tired, on account of the strong opposition met with, and you then dropped back into the current of the old conditions and if anything became more helpless than you were before.

Others may have heard of the saying, but it did not impress them; for they could not accept the assertion that any of the inharmonies in their lives are the result of their own beliefs, or of their past thinking crystallized into beliefs. They preferred to blame it all on someone else, and even God came in for a share of the blame.

The main trouble with almost everyone is that they do not realize how many negative and destructive beliefs they are carrying around with them in the subconscious realms of mind and which creep through into the conscious mind whenever it is free from interest in other things.

Until you can begin to study your mind and watch for and note these negative beliefs when they come and you will find that they are actually beliefs and refuse them further support, there is not much hope for you.

In fact it is the first thing you must learn to do. Those who are too mentally lazy to do such watching and controlling of their thoughts, are usually the ones who will not accept that their own thinking and beliefs create for them all of the conditions now manifesting in their lives.

But it makes no difference whether you accept it as being true or not; it is the law.

I. THE LAW

Now if you are ready to hear the law, we will state it in words that everyone can understand.

Note these words, and let them impress themselves on you, so that from this moment ever afterward they will live in your mind as a guiding influence.

"WHATEVER YOU THINK AND HOLD IN CONSCIOUSNESS AS BEING SO, OUT MANIFESTS ITSELF IN YOUR BODY OR AFFAIRS."

Whether you accept this as yet or not, consider for a while the truth that every thought you think, especially those relating in any way to self, hovers around in your mental atmosphere, just as a child stays close to its parent. These thoughts being about yourself receive the life that maintains them from the feeling that you put into them.

In other words, the thoughts themselves are but mental forms, but when you think them with feeling of any kind you fill these forms with life and they become as living things which ever return to you, their parent, to be fed with more living power. For all feeling expressed is life, is vital power, and if you only knew it, all the thoughts which persistently influence your mind and harass you, are only your mental children clamoring for food and attention, and compelling more worrying, anxiety, or fear from you; all of which are excellent food containing rich vital power, and which makes them grow rapidly, until they become so powerful that in time they dominate your mind so that you can scarcely think of anything else.

When the fact is, these thoughts exist to you only when you let them into your mind that is, they are of importance to you only when you give them attention and recognition, But on the other hand, their power over you and their life can quickly be nullified by simply knowing the law, and refusing to feed them longer with life power by giving them further attention or interest, And it should not be necessary to state that voicing such thoughts definitely and speedily outmanifests them, for the spoken word is far more potent than the thought. Above all else you should guard carefully your speech, voicing nothing you do not want to see manifest. Always remember, however, that by preventing such thoughts entering the mind there will be no impulse to voice them.

So that you can see now that it is all a matter of consciousness, of thinking and harboring the right kind of thoughts those you wish to outmanifest, and of letting into your mind no thoughts you do not want to manifest in your body or affairs.

And perhaps you can also see that what is ordinarily called thinking is only the admitting into your mind of thoughts that originated chiefly in other minds and which you of course attracted to you. This is also true of all negative, inharmonious and destructive thoughts; there must be something in you that attracts them or they would not come.

Many will still permit them to come, for only by the suffering, hardship and struggle to escape from their influence that you undergo, will you learn how to free yourself and gain the power to control and consciously direct your life to constructive ends.

That is the hard way, but we are now going to show you the true way to free yourself forever from fear and worry about finances, and from all other destructive forces.

We are assuming that all who read are students and followers of Christ's teachings. You remember those significant words of His in the Sermon on the Mount.

"Take no thought (or be not anxious) saying, what shall we eat, or what shall we drink, or with what shall we be clothed; for your heavenly Father knows that you have need of all these things. But seek first the Kingdom (Consciousness) of God, and His righteousness (Right Ideas); and all these things will be added unto you."

We know that those words seem important to you, but we also know that very few take them as actual promises and try definitely and determinedly to put them to the proof.

But that is the very thing you must do, if you would obey the law; and when we show you how to free yourself from fear and worry you will not only be able to free yourself from the power money has over you, but you will have found the straight and narrow way to the Kingdom. And all the powers of the Kingdom will help you, if you are strong and determined enough to win the goal. For the Kingdom of God and His righteousness is only a state of consciousness where we do right thinking where we think God's thoughts only.

Can you do that? Surely you can if you will. Then this is the way: THE WAY you must train yourself to STAND GUARD CONTINUALLY AT THE DOOR OF YOUR MIND, AND TO LET IN NO THOUGHTS OR FEELINGS THAT YOU DO NOT WANT TO OUTMANIFEST.

Think this over carefully, and you will see that it is the only way.

It may seem hard at first, and you may not know what to admit and what to deny.

But guard the door from every negative thought and feeling of whatsoever nature from every thought that you know God would not have you think; from every doubt, fear, worry, anxiety, or concern of any kind; from every tendency to criticize, judge or condemn anybody or anything or any condition; from self pity, jealousy, envy, irritation, unkindness, anger, hatred, etc. These will give you an idea of what are negative and ungodlike thoughts, and which must no longer have a part in your consciousness.

If you will keep all such untrue thoughts out of your mind, you can see that then and then only can your Higher Self draw into your mind the true and positive thoughts that will attract to you the good that is waiting to manifest itself to you. For while your mind is cluttered with all those fearful, worrying, discouraged, sick, weak, poverty-tainted thoughts, how can you expect anyone who feels these vibrations and vibrations are things you cannot cover up to be attracted to you, or how can you expect God to inspire you with thoughts of a beneficial nature?

In fact, such negative thoughts actually keep away the things you are longing to have manifest in your life for like attracts like.

Think! Poverty-stricken thoughts do not attract prosperity or jobs; sick thoughts do not build a healthy consciousness; and belief that you are a failure invites failure.

You say this all sounds good, but when one is sunk so deep in conditions that no matter which way he turns he sees only sickness, hunger, poverty or failure facing him, despite months of effort to conquer the condition, to get work, or to do something to tide over till better days come, how is he to think of any thing else?

Yes, dear friend, we see what you are up against, but we also see that you are caught fast between the horns of a dilemma. You have sought help from the world of men and it has turned you down. You have exhausted all the forces of self, and you admit that you are completely helpless. And perhaps you have even prayed to God, and seemingly He has not heard, or He has not answered you.

But where is this God to whom you have prayed? Is he somewhere up in the skies, or in some hazy place, you know not where?

Have you prayed to God within you? Have you turned there and opened your heart to Him, deep within your self, in the Kingdom, where your Higher Self abides?

If not, dear friend, then after reading this article carefully until you truly get its full meaning for you, pray to Him there; get down on your knees and in deep and true humility pour out your heart to Him, knowing that He as your Higher Self hears you, that He does know that you have need of all these things, and that He will answer you.

Go back to those words in the Sermon on the Mount and read them over again and again, until you get all of their wondrous meaning and realize that they are meant for you, and that they are a definite promise made by the Master to you that if you will do what you are there told to do, the Father will give to you all things that you need. Think! This is Jesus' promise to you, and therefore it will be fulfilled if you do your part.

YOU CAN DO IT. You can do it, you must do it if you would have the blessings which He promises you, and which we promise you when we say that you can have an abundance of all good things and that you can be free from the dominance of money forever.

And what must you do? You must not be anxious or worry anymore about what you shall eat or drink or what you shall wear, for your loving Father knows that you must have all of these things. But if you will seek first His Kingdom that is, His Consciousness, where you must think only His thoughts for you as we have shown you how to do, and then will do what He tells you to do when His thoughts come into your mind, He will provide you with all the good things He has had in store for you from the beginning.

We know that we are telling you to do what now seems almost impossible. But, dear friend, this is the only way to win these blessings; and you say you will do anything to obtain them, if it is humanly possible.

It is not only possible, but it is the very thing ordained and intended for you by your Higher Self or He would not have brought this message to you and placed this ultimatum so squarely before you. You have tried your way, and you have tried the world's way, and you know where they have brought you. And now you are given the opportunity of trying God's way!

The way laid out for you in the beginning. Can you not see that it is now the only way out for you? Thus God brings His children that love Him finally to realize that they cannot serve both God and Mammon. For they must be shown or that they are serving Mammon just as much by fearing him and yielding to the power of be money, as they would be by openly worshipping money and becoming its slave when having great quantities of it.

They must be made to see that by fearing money's seeming power they are making it first and God second in on their lives, and until they truly want to serve God more than any other thing, and prove it by their right thinking, speech and action, they are not yet where His help can reach them.

II. THE ULTIMATUM

So this is the ultimatum that you are facing. You have now come to the place where God holds out His hand to you, and says: "My child, I would help you. But it means that you must give yourself and your ideas over wholly to Me, must learn to think only My thoughts, speak only what I would say, and do only what I would have you to do. It means that you must not let into your mind or believe any other thoughts, no matter what appearances are or how much such thoughts beg for admittance.

You have had your chance and you see what a sorry mess you have made of things.

Now if you are willing utterly and completely to trust Me, and to wait upon and serve Me only, and will keep your mind and heart clean and empty of all untrue thoughts so that I may fill them with My thoughts, I will inspire in you the ideas that will lift you quickly out of your present consciousness, which means out of present conditions into one where peace, harmony and plenty will be your mental children, that will ever come to you to be fed with loving trust in Me, confidence in your power to express Me, and with the pure joy of living, that you will then be feeling as the natural and continuous state of your consciousness.

Is this worth trying for? Do you really want it? Then what are you going to do about it? If you are willing to make a supreme effort and to put all the power of your will into it; will make yourself a positive agent of your Father's Will, looking only and always to Him to guide and inspire you, you will truly receive all the help you need, and will find, if you persist despite any discouragements that may come testing your determination, that you will then walk straight into the good that has long been waiting for you.

III. APPEARANCES

This means that from this moment you must pay no more attention to appearances, for what is now appearing is but the outmanifestation of what you formerly visualized in your thinking, and which your fearing and worrying crystallized into facts and fastened upon you.

Try to realize the great significance of this.

It is not what you see as conditions surrounding you that really counts, it is what you believe is so. And when you know as we have proven to you that what you believe is the cause of what is manifesting outwardly as it now appears, you will definitely begin to change your beliefs into those you want to manifest.

Think this over, for it is the only way you can change conditions and their appearances, you must remove from your consciousness the beliefs you are holding there, by replacing them with beliefs you want to see manifest in your life and affairs.

How can you do this when you cannot help but believe the things that stare you in the face, no matter which way you turn?

IV. THE WAY OUT

We will now show you the way, a way so simple and easy that anyone can do it, if they will obey exactly what we tell them to do. All that is needed is to say over and over again to yourself until you believe it absolutely, letting not a single doubt of its truth ever enter your mind, the following words.

"GOD LOVES AND CARES FOR ME AND IS GIVING ME ALL GOOD THINGS.

I LOVE HIM AND THINK HIS THOUGHTS AND DO ONLY THE THINGS HE WANTS ME TO DO."

Try to realize the full truth of these words to feel it, to see yourself actually living in the consciousness of it, going about your daily work in that consciousness. If you do this, it will bring the greatest possible blessings into your life. The first statement should not be hard to believe, for you surely know that He loves and cares for you; for whether you know it yet or not, everything that has come into your life has been good for you, for through these things He has brought you to the place where you should be willing to look to and trust Him only, so that His love and care can give you all the good things He has had for you from the beginning.

And it should be easy to love Him, and through consciously loving and trying to think His thoughts, you can see that it opens your mind so that His thoughts come into it, and can thus direct you just what to do that will bring success, prosperity, health, harmony and happiness into your life.

Dear friends, we wish that we could reveal the truth of the above wonderful statements so clearly to you that they will live with you and will motivate your every thought, word and act forever afterward. They are so mighty in their truth that if lived they will make you more than man.

So do not pass them by because they seem so simple and commonplace. Stay with them until all their glorious import dawns upon to you and you feel the change that they will surely and quickly bring into your consciousness and therefore into your life and all your affairs.

V. DEFINITE INSTRUCTIONS

And now for instructions of a concrete nature. Let us take some definite good that you want to have manifest in your life. We do not mean things, but conditions that will bring harmony and happiness to yourself and dear ones; which means that you must make sure that it is good, that it is what the God you wants you to have. That should be easy, for He has ordained all good things for you, but you must know that and be able to see it as good. Then build in your mind a picture of that good.

Build it perfect, in every detail, so that it stands out clear and distinct as a finished and accomplished fact. According to how complete and distinct is this picture in your mind is it actually finished on the mental plane - the plane of concrete mental forms, which determines its physical appearance - and is it ready to come forth into manifestation.

And now if you will follow exactly the same process which brought into manifestation all of the present unwanted conditions in your life, only using the opposite kind of thoughts and feelings, as we shall indicate, you can bring forth into perfect manifestation this picture now existing on the mental plane awaiting the action of your will.

We will take as an illustration a friend who recently lost her position. Several weeks before, this friend mentioned to the writer that their business was very poor and that they had laid off several who had charge of departments similar to hers, and she supposed she would be the next to go. The writer remonstrated with her and tried to show that that attitude of mind would bring to her what she did not want.

Two weeks later another friend reported that she had said the same thing to her, and we do not know to how many others she had voiced it. But a few days afterward, as she had pictured it, the notice of her dismissal came.

Now let us analyze the mental process which created and brought to pass the losing of her position. The conditions of the business, the letting go of other department heads and clerks naturally caused our friend to build a picture in her mind of her also probably having to go sooner or later, and through the fear of it she actually saw herself leaving. Day after day the conditions in the office, her talks with fellow employees and with others in other businesses in similar bad straits, and with those who had lost their jobs, increased and intensified her fear and helped her to build in the details of her picture, until she had it all finished and perfect. Then she naturally felt she would soon have to go. So of course it had to come to pass.

Now do you understand? The proof that she and she alone created the necessity of her going was,

1. she was the last of all the heads of departments let go, for she was the most efficient;

2. she began criticizing her employers and their actions;

3. she learned afterward that they did not want to lose her and they might give her back her position, having hired two young men to replace the other women let go.

But she had created on the mental plane the finished thought form of being dismissed and had vitalized it with her fears and other feelings, and as a result that thought form had to outmanifest; and so it forced itself into the minds of her employers and impelled them to do what they otherwise would not have done.

Now let us apply similar thought processes to the bringing forth of the good you pictured above into manifestation.

You have built and now see the finished picture of that good, but now instead of seeing a negative outmanifestation of that picture, we will see a positive and happy one.

So every day and as often as possible during the day you will see your pictured good manifesting, affecting your life in every way you can visualize it; see yourself actually enjoying it and sharing it with your dear ones and friends; and all the time you are seeing it consciously pouring deep feelings of joy, of love and gratitude into your sense of its being an actual and living reality, your own creation, the product of your own spirit, which you are nursing and bringing forth into physical being.

And just as surely as our friend brought forth her unwanted creation into actuality, so must your good come forth and be to you all that you visioned and intended it to be. It is the law, and a faithful following of this process in all constructive thinking and creating will always bring the results sought, even as your destructive thinking brought the results unsought.

Study the above examples and explanation until the process stands out clear and true to you. Then study your own individual case, until you see plainly how you came to your present state. Then begin to reverse your thought processes as shown above, until you express along constructive lines only. Your sincere desire to free yourself - not just to ease yourself from suffering and hardship, but to know the truth, to learn the cause of being in any unwanted condition, and to gain the ability to free yourself from it, so you can help others to get free will draw to you the help needed, and you will in time be free.

Do not give up if your mind does not respond immediately, for it has formed the habit of wrong seeing and thinking, and you were a long time forming present conditions. Just know that if you persist until your mind sees that you are determined and really mean it, it will soon fall in line and follow the new ways of thinking you lay down for it as easily as it did the old ways in the past.

The main thing is to remember always that you are dealing and working with mental substance on the mental plane, and are not concerned with outer appearances and conditions, for you know that by such work you are shaping and changing conditions to those you wish to be manifest.

We have now shown you the Law. We have explained to you its operation. We have made clear that by wrong thinking and believing you have brought upon yourself the conditions now surrounding you, and we have shown you how to free yourself from these conditions and how to create those you wish to manifest in your life. There now remain only a few more things to tell you to help impress it all upon your mind so that it will become a part of your consciousness.

VI. BE POSITIVE

The first is the importance of always being positive in your thinking, positive in your speaking, and positive in your doing. And never negative. The negative person attracts all the negative things of life, all the inharmonies, troubles that are in the mental atmosphere -the effluvia of other weak and negative minds; while a positive person attracts all the good. If you understand the radio you will know that when you set your dial at a certain wave length, all that is "on the air" of that wave length will make itself heard.

It is exactly the same with your mind; it will receive whatever happens to be "on the air" of the wave length to which your thoughts are attuned. So that it is "up to you" and you only what your mind radio gives forth or outmanifests.

Have you ever noticed how a positive person in a crowd of ordinary persons is always the center of attraction, always makes his or her presence felt, and always accomplishes things that lesser ones never think of? A most forcible illustration was once when driving on a thoroughfare where there was a temporary narrow road built at the side of where a new bridge was being constructed. We came to a halt because of a long line of automobiles ahead. After waiting for some minutes, the writer got out and noticed perhaps thirty cars on the long decline to the bottom of the ravine and a similar line up the hill on the other side. But seemingly the left side of the road was clear all through. He could not see any sense in waiting, so he pulled out and started ahead and went through without opposition. While going up the other side he looked back and found a grcat string of cars following him, and a man in one of these told him that they had been waiting back there for twenty minutes.

Evidently two cars from opposite directions had come together with others following them, and they were afraid they could not get through on the narrow road, because of other cars coming. It is always so in life; the positive soul gets there, the negative one stays behind, or tags along when he finds a leader. Why be negative? It is all an attitude of mind, and can be changed simply by changing your beliefs.

Besides we are all sons and daughters of God, children of the greatest King in the world, Who naturally gives all the riches and good things of His Kingdom to all those of us who know it is our divine heritage and who will accept and enjoy them.

VII. A KING'S SON

Try to realize that you are the equal - nay the superior - of any world Prince, the son of the King of any World Kingdom; for our Father's Kingdom includes his father's kingdom; and if we could lift our minds to the consciousness of our true Selves as Sons of God, we would go about KNOWING that all that our Father, the King, has is ours, and that all of the Father's servants will rush to supply to anticipate our every need. This is actually so. Each one can experience it. All you need is to believe it, and to go about in that consciousness, even as does the Prince of any world kingdom in his lesser kingdom consciousness.

Then as a King's son YOU must learn, if all that your Father has is yours, to spend freely of the riches He has given you with absolute fearlessness. For there is no limit to them, no lack of wealth, for it is always available. His resources are inexhaustible.

You must acquire this consciousness, you must feel even as does the other Prince about spending or using money Think you that he has any fear of lack or limitation of supply?

No, there is always a great plenty for his every need, for his every comfort, every pleasure, for every constructive idea; for he knows that back of him is his father, the King, and all the resources of his kingdom. So must you learn to know that back of you is your Father God, with all the resources of His Kingdom.

VIII. USE MONEY FEARLESSLY

The quickest way to rid your mind of that old fear of want, fear of your job, fear of the power of money, is to have an absolute trust in your heavenly Father's loving care and for you to pay out gladly your last dollar for a needed thing, KNOWING that by so doing you make it possible for Him to supply you with plenty more.

It is as if your needs must keep the stream of money ever flowing, if you would not clog up its source. For money, in its true sense, is the means for the perfect expression of material life; even as the blood is the means for the perfect expression of physical health.

In both cases your mind must not only hold true and pure thoughts God's thoughts only about the material life of yourself and others, and about your physical well-being, but you must know that God's Mind is the Source of all true thoughts; and by perfect faith and trust in Him you thus keep your self open to the free circulation of His Thoughts in your consciousness about both your affairs and your body, thus creating perfect health and harmony in both.

This has been proven by many so-called "tithers". They have created a consciousness where they know that, by using money freely in such perfect trust in God, and especially in thanksgiving and loving gratitude to Him, giving freely a percentage of their income to that part of His Work which is bringing the Truth to them, they become greatly blessed in this world's goods and are put in a position where they can help many souls to come into this same truth.

It is the pinching and holding on to your last dollar, fearing that no more will come, that actually prevents your receiving more.

For giving, more than anything else, helps to open the channel so that supply, both spiritual and material, can freely flow.

Now we wish finally to emphasize that the application and proving of this great law not only will bring financial freedom and success, but it will bring also perfect health, harmony, and happiness into all departments of your life. For when you begin to think only true thoughts about yourself, then of course God's consciousness lives in your body and His thoughts rule your mind, and there can manifest only perfect health in your body and perfect harmony in all your various affairs; when naturally happiness must sing in your heart and be your daily companion.

So, dear friend, we have given you this message - one born of an intense yearning to furnish to those who are wandering in the darkness of present world conditions a sure guide to lead them back into the Light of Love, of abiding Trust, and of true Happiness.

THE END

BOOK THREE
THE WAY BEYOND

PREFACE

In our booklet, "THE WAY OUT" was pointed the way to freedom from lack, limitation, inharmony, disease and unhappiness, and there is no excuse for any who faithfully follow the suggestions given to be any longer in such condition.

The booklet has reached scores of thousands of readers and many have been lifted by its truths into a new consciousness, and thereby into a new world, where everything and everybody are changed, for they are seeing with new eyes, and with different understanding.

That which appears is no longer what it seemed, but the good and the real are now visible and can be seen shining through all conditions and people -because they are now looked for, and the former negative tendencies are tabooed and not allowed to enter the consciousness.

This is not the case with all of course, for a great number have not been able to conquer those tendencies which so long have been permitted to rule. The press of circumstances and the negative conditions everywhere manifest seemingly have been too much for them and they have become utterly discouraged, not knowing that they actually have within themselves the power to rise out of these conditions, and that help is waiting the moment they awaken from their despondency and definitely determine to do the best they can to prove the truth of what was stated in the booklet.

It is for such that this new Message is written, with the earnest desire that all who read will be so inspired by its truths that they will make the necessary effort and will thus receive the good that has been waiting for them from the beginning.

We first urge that everyone who reads procure a copy of "THE WAY OUT", if one is not already owned, and that it be studied carefully and prayerfully. It will do no good merely to read it, even to study it, unless what is given you to do is faithfully TRIED until proven -that is, tried day after day in all your thinking, speaking and acting, for at least one month.

If you will do it that long, we promise that such a change will manifest in your consciousness and likewise in your affairs that it will be a turning point in your life, and you will never again return to the old way of thinking and acting. Is it not then worth the effort? Then do not let anything prevent your making a supreme effort, asking God to give you the strength and ability to accomplish what we have shown.

I. GOD WITHIN YOU

Now, we are going to try to make clear to you the statement in "THE WAY OUT" that God is within you; make it so clear that never more will you think of Him as somewhere up in the skies, nor will you be uncertain as to who or what He is,

First try to realize that the life animating and growing you is not your life, that you have no control over it, that it does things to you, causes you to do things, puts you through all the experiences you are undergoing without your consent, and that seemingly it knows just what it is doing and must have a very wise and loving purpose in doing it.

Likewise the consciousness that you call yours seemingly receives all its ideas, thoughts and impressions wholly independently of your will or desire, They come into your mind when they will, influence your feelings and actions continually, and you have little power to prevent it,

Also you will admit that you have no power of your own, that you can think, speak and do only as the power to do these things is given you from within, and that Something doing all this, unquestionably is a greater, far wiser and a very loving Something that knows always what to do, knows the end before the beginning, and is apparently trying to teach your human mind about itself, teach it the lessons contained in each experience, and the laws back of life and of physical manifestation. Because that Something is so different from and yet is so intimate a part of what you call you, it must be akin to what is termed God.

We have called it the Higher Self, and it is in fact very God in you. It is like a ray or reflection of God's mind shining somewhere deep within your consciousness, a "light which shineth in the darkness, but the darkness (of the outer human mind) knoweth it not".

For certainly when It can get your mind's attention and you listen, it displays a wisdom that is as near to that of God as the human mind can conceive. And those who heed and obey are given a glimpse of something wonderful, which while inexpressible is altogether divine and most satisfying.

II. GOD IS ALL IN ALL

You have heard the statement that God is All in All, and of "the light which lighteth every man that cometh into the world". Then that light must be a ray of God's Mind that shines in the darkness of the human mind, ever trying to make it aware of its Divine Source within itself - the Mind of God, from which it derives all that it is, all that it has, and all power to be, to know or to do anything.

Then think, if God is All in All, He is in everything and in everybody -no matter what it is or who he is. It must be so! Yet who of us always sees and acknowledges Him in such?

And because we do not acknowledge Him in His manifestations, refuse to see Him, and call Him everything He is not, we see instead all the error, the evil and the lies that our darkened minds have accepted as real, lose ourselves in the maze of our "separate" misconceptions; and in consequence endure the inharmonies, disease and suffering of minds thinking themselves apart from the Consciousness that includes them and all that is.

God being All in All, then all things and all men are good and perfect. They could not be otherwise, when God and His goodness and perfection are everywhere.

But make no mistake, when stating that all things and all men are good and perfect, we are not speaking of what you with your "separate" mind and present understanding see and believe; we are not speaking of "appearances" - of your separate mind's creations.

For what you see now are only the pictures you have built in your mind of what you thought was the truth - before you really knew about God's being All in All and ever showing forth His goodness, beauty and perfection in everything - to those who have eyes to see.

Therefore it is necessary first to convince your mind of the truth, so that it can be free itself of all these untrue beliefs - these false pictures of

God and of His expressions of Himself that it has built and is carrying around in its consciousness.

Then listen! God, Who is All in All and Who is all good and all perfect, must be also all wise, all loving and all powerful. Anything less than these is not of God, but must be man's wrong, ignorant, and distorted concepts of God and of His expressions of Himself.

Think that out until you see how true it is.

Then all things of an inharmonious or unhappy nature that you see, whatever they be that are less than good or perfect, are only what you think is so, because of ignorance or wrong teaching, And so long as you continue to believe these things are real, they will continue to be real to you, no matter what they are, whether they pertain to the conditions surrounding you, to your body, to your self, to your affairs, or to those invisible things which relate to and affect your life, health and happiness.

III. GOD IS THE REAL YOU

Now let us relate this truth of God being All in All to yourself. If He is all we have stated, then He must be the real you, must be that higher, greater you we pointed out earlier in this message, whose life is illuminating your body, whose mind is influencing all your thoughts, speech and actions, and whose power enables you to do all things that you do.

It must then be His Consciousness that is your consciousness, but stepped down through your Higher Self to your soul and then to your human mind, expressing itself on the Spiritual plane in your Higher Self as the Christ Consciousness, on the soul plane in your soul or soul consciousness, and on the physical plane in your brain mind as mortal consciousness.

But it is all God's Consciousness relayed down through your Higher Self, and enabling you to be as much aware of God, the Real Self of you and the One Self of all men (for is He not All in All?) as the channel of your darkened mortal mind has been illumined to perceive Him and to partake of His Consciousness.

It is said that to Know God, man must first know his self. And when you truly know that you are not a thing of flesh and blood, but are a human soul or a center of consciousness, clothed by a garment of flesh, even as your soul clothes your Real or Christ Self, the Holy Spirit or Consciousness of God as we have shown above, you can begin to understand how God actually is within you - IS you.

Now let us consider you first as a soul, a center of consciousness, and then we will try to show you the relation of your soul to your human mind and your Higher, Spiritual Self.

You in your integrity are a soul and are pure consciousness, in other words you are that which is conscious or aware of all that comes to you from without through the avenue of your five senses, or through vibrations which they are not sensitive enough to perceive, such as impressions or thoughts from other centers of consciousness. All of these sensations are brought to your consciousness through the mediumship of your human mind, while the vibrations mentioned are received directly by the soul and are interpreted to the mind according to how the mind has been prepared to understand them.

As a soul or consciousness you are distinct from your human mind, for the mind serves merely as an instrument to receive and inform you of what comes from without in the world of matter.

Yet your mind is in reality an outer extension of your soul consciousness, slowed down to the mental capacity of your human brain, there serving as your agent in the informing you of all things going on in the physical world and the carrying out of your instructions pertaining to that world.

In that partial and necessarily limited consciousness, your mind grew to think itself a self and separate from you in your soul consciousness. In this fancied separateness it gradually filled its consciousness with all those wrong concepts and beliefs about physical and mental things spoken of above, which grew so real and tangible in its consciousness that they in time ruled all your thoughts, speech and actions. And this outer and fancied separate consciousness is what constitutes your lower or mortal self.

But these concepts and beliefs should have no influence over your soul consciousness only as you let them. The proof is, when you get quiet and still your mind and shut out all thoughts and impressions coming from without, then you are in your pure soul consciousness and are free to be aware of the impressions coming from within your soul.

For then you learn that deep within the soul there is a higher consciousness and a Spiritual intelligence that presses the soul from within informing you of Spiritual things, even as the outer mind's consciousness presses from without to inform you of material things.

And that higher or innermost consciousness is that of your Higher or Divine Self.

In reality there is only one Self, but this enables you to see how the Higher Self, the Spirit of God in man, reaches down or out from the center of man's being in Divine Consciousness into the soul consciousness, and thence outward into the mortal mind, giving to man's brain its consciousness, which causes man to think his consciousness separate, when it is only the consciousness of God thinned down to the brain mind's capacity to hold and use it.

IV. YOUR GOD SELF

Then the Higher Self, this Spirit of God deep within you, is the real you, is the Self that has ever been directing all the activities of your life, has been actually doing all through you, knows just what He is doing, assumes a responsibility and evidently sees the end before the beginning.

Then you can realize that of your human self you do nothing, and never did anything; that all the power, knowledge and life you have comes from your Higher Self; and that if you ever wish to be, to do, or to have anything, and to gain the freedom, happiness and peace your soul seeks, it behooves you to get well acquainted with that Self, to learn to cooperate with Him, and to wait upon and serve Him in all the activities of your life.

From this you can also realize that the reason you failed to gain any of these things in the past, is because you tried to get them without reckoning upon your Higher Self or knowing His part in the doing - you tried to do it alone. So He let you fail again and again, until you came to that place where you learned the uselessness of trying to do anything yourself, and you became willing to turn to Him and humbly ask Him to take charge and you gladly yielded over all to Him and put all your trust in Him.

Everyone must come to that place - every seeker of the true way of life; for until self with its human mind has been completely humbled and gives up utterly, it cannot accept the truth of its non-reality and of the actuality of the God-man within, and that He can do all and will provide all things - when the human mind yields itself wholly to Him.

If you who read have come to that place, and are truly ready to give yourself to the God Self within, then we will tell you of a great but simple law that you must follow.

V. A SIMPLE LAW

That Law is "Whatever is before you to do, do it the best you know how, in order to please your God-Self". For He placed you just where you now are and provided the particular task confronting you as the best means and opportunity in which to teach your human mind the next lessons you are to learn, and to develop in you the spiritual qualities you still lack in order to make your human self a perfect instrument for His use.

Then in doing that task, for He provides all tasks and brings you to all problems, having now given yourself over wholly to Him, you are concerned only that you do what is before you the best you can, KNOWING that He will provide the power, understanding and ability needed, and that you are not responsible any more for results, as they are all in His keeping. For have you not put the full responsibility on Him, are now trusting everything to Him, and consequently you no longer have any fears, doubts or worries to clog your mind and prevent His accomplishing His purpose for you? Only by thus yielding all to Him can you be a clean and open channel through which He can bring through into being the good and perfect things He intends to manifest in your life. For He can intend nothing less than that, else why all the trouble He is taking with you?

It is all a matter of trusting, dear friend, of trusting the God within you. If you have failed in the past, no matter how hard you tried, it is because you did not trust enough.

Therefore, we are bringing this great truth closer by asking you truly to trust the God within, your Higher Self, the Christ of you, Who we have shown has all the wisdom and power of God; to let go utterly and put ALL your trust in Him.

You must learn thus to trust, until it becomes the supreme and dominant influence in your consciousness, for THE ONLY THING THAT PREVENTS YOUR GOOD FROM COMING INTO NATURAL

AND CONTINUOUS EXPRESSION IS YOUR LACK OF REAL FAITH AND TRUST IN THE GOD WITHIN YOU YOUR CHRIST SELF.

This means that if instead of faith and trust you still let fears, doubts and worries in to your mind, then of course there they cause you to build negative pictures of the things you are fearing, and you proceed to entertain and feed them by further fears, until they become actual living things in your mental world. In time they largely control your mind and you are helpless. And naturally every time you succumb to them, you grow more helpless.

Is this not true? -Then what is the solution? Only one thing. You must let go completely and turn the whole problem over to God. Do that actually -"wash your hands" of it, "step out from under," and throw the entire responsibility upon Him.

Think! Can you do that? Try it. In fact, He wants you to do it. Talk to this God within the Real Self of you, and tell Him that you are through, that you have done your best, and that is all you can do -and it was useless. And now it is up to Him; He will have to handle it. Actually mean it, and then let go and truly "wash your hands" of an responsibility.

Then, and not until then, has He got your mind in the state where it is ready to hear His Voice and learn what He has in store for you.

For once it has really thrown off the burden of self, there is no longer a negative force attracting the old fears, doubts and worries.

Instead you become a positive force in your believing that He now will take care of all things, for you intend to do nothing and to give Him the chance to prove what He can do.

VI. AN ABSOLUTE LETTING GO

It is to just that state of mind He desires to bring you, where you actually let go, giving the load you are carrying over to Him, and thereby become as free as a little child, just such a child as we will now picture to you.

Standing on the sidewalk of a busy street waiting for the light signal, is a little boy of three years whose hand is tightly clasped in that of his father. Then they start across. Is the child frightened by the big automobiles and the noise and tumult at this busy corner? No, he sees and knows no danger and gleefully enjoys the turmoil and the mixing with the crowd hurrying across --for he knows that Dad is taking care of him and will not let any harm come to him. Just as he unconsciously knows that Dad will feed and clothe him, for to him Dad is as God who will provide everything he needs and take every care of him.

Think you your God-Self does not love you and is not taking equal care of you, His child? For are you not a part of His Being and does He not need you to express His Self?

Then how could He let you really suffer or come to any harm? What your human mind suffers and the dangers it fears are only the nightmares of childhood which disappear when the light of understanding is brought.

Besides such mental suffering actually burns away the qualities of self that hinder His perfect expression, while through the fears that come and persist He teaches you how to become strong.

It is these mental fears for they are purely mental, that is, they exist in your mind, not in His Consciousness that are clogging your mind-channel, and preventing His pouring through it the good that awaits.

Then you will have to cleanse your mind of all such negative things - of every doubt, fear or worry, and especially of those wrong pictures you are carrying around in your consciousness. Do you still see yourself as sick, or ailing, or poor, or very much needing anything? Then can you not realize it is that picture which is clogging up the channel? For what you think and carry around in consciousness as being so always out-manifests itself. How can the good you wish to manifest get by that picture?

That is the whole trouble, dear friend, you have not cleansed your mind of those old picture-beliefs, some of which are hiding down in the dark corners of your subconsciousness, purposely refusing to come out into the light; for they know, the moment you see them for what they are, their days are numbered. In fact, you must go down into the subconsciousness and dig out all of such and cast them forth; for until the whole mind is clean and free of all negative and untrue thoughts and feelings and is kept so, it cannot be brought into your God Consciousness where there are only positive, true, good and perfect ideas about you and you can see all things in their reality, even as He sees, and you can know as He knows; your mind thus becoming a perfect channel through which He can give you your divine heritage which He has so long had waiting for you.

VII. IMAGINE THE GOD-YOU

Now we ask you to try to imagine yourself in the Consciousness of your God-Self and to see with His eyes this self you call you, and the other selves around you and the world you live in.

In the first place, know that as He is all wise, all loving and all powerful, and is still you, but a perfect you, He must have a perfect mind and body -but not like your physical self. His body is that "image and likeness of God" in which man was originally formed. And if God made man like Himself, who could change man's perfect being? Not even man, himself.

Then man must still be perfect! Yes, it cannot be otherwise. For think you anyone could alter or bring to naught any perfect thing God created?

We know you are asking how then did man become so changed. He is not changed -the real man. He is your Higher Self - the Real You - the perfect Man, just as God created him, as He now sees him, and as he will always be.

Now listen! What you and others see are mortal man's creations - not God's. They are merely the creations of man's fancied "separate" mind, and have no existence except in his brain-mind's consciousness. When God gave man free-will, He gave him the power to think as he wills, which means to create.

He could think good -God's thoughts, or evil- not God's thoughts. Man did not realize his God nature then; he had only his human nature to judge by, and the only way to learn was, not by taking God's or anyone's word for things, but by thinking, by trying and finding what his creations - the things, conditions and people of his world - were not.

And so he thought and created and tried from the beginning to make perfect things and conditions in this world of his consciousness with the results you see everywhere about you.

Not that many men back through the ages have not learned the truth - the truth we are trying to teach you, -that they can do nothing of themselves, but with the help of the God within them they can do all things, can have all things, can be all things. And with His help such have come into and are now dwelling in their Christ Consciousness, are One with Him, and are doing the Father s Work on earth even as others are doing it in Heaven.

VIII. THE CHRIST CONSCIOUSNESS

And what do they see in this Consciousness? They see that they are souls, living in a perfect world, where every soul is young, good, beautiful and perfect, even as the Father conceived them, and where everything is devised for the free use and enjoyment of its inhabitants. Which means that there is a rich abundance of all good things for everyone always available. No one there ever needs anything, for it is always at hand. There any desired thing is created by thought and you can have it when and as you wish it. Then of course no one takes from another or owes another anything, for everyone has everything he wants; because all he has to do is to see clearly in his mind what he wants and it takes shape and substance right before his eyes, ready and perfect for his use.

From this you can see there is no selfishness there, for all there are those in whom self no longer is. There is no injustice, for the law of justice rules everyone's consciousness.

There is no evil, for it has been learned that evil, sin, sickness, inharmony, and unhappiness are the creations of mortal mind, and of course one who is selfless is in his Christ Consciousness and no longer thinks and thereby creates such things.

Does this help you to see how and why man is responsible for this outer world that it is his own creation, and not God's creation?

And can you now see what is God's world, His Kingdom, your heavenly home, where you can return as a Prodigal Son anytime you will be remembering and seeing only the truth, and where you will find your heavenly Father waiting for you with outstretched arms.

And Who is this heavenly Father? He is your own Real Self, the God-You, that is always back in that Consciousness deep within your soul, where you can retire any moment you will. All you have to do is to throw off everything that presses upon your consciousness from the outer world of the human mind and turn your attention to the inner world of Spirit. Especially must you refuse to see, to talk about, or let your mind dwell upon outer conditions, no matter how hard they appear or how they seemingly affect you; for remember they exist only in the world of man's mind, and not in the real world the God-You sees and lives in.

If you resolutely do this, it will not be long before you will have evidence of the reality of this Kingdom within, and you will hear His

Voice and receive definite guidance as to what He wills and what is His purpose for you. For He must have a purpose, or why all this disciplining and developing of your mind and character?

Make no mistake, He knows what He is doing and why; and when you have given self entirely over to Him, He will take you into His Consciousness, and there you will work with Him to accomplish what He intended from the beginning.

The beautiful part of it is that there are others there working with you, others who have found Him within themselves, have found there a new and wonderful self, a wonderful world, and wonderful comrades in it; a world far more real than the ever-changing one of their own creation.

Yes, they have found their eternal home, the Kingdom of God's Consciousness, the same home which Jesus described in His many parables, when trying to tell of it to the people of His day, where He went after His mission was accomplished; where He now lives and works among His disciples who have followed Him there.

To them He is a very real and actual Teacher, Guide and Friend, Who is preparing them for the great day when He will make Himself manifest to all His followers on earth and will bring Heaven down to earth to be truly in the midst of men.

IX. THE NEXT STEP

This shows you what is possible to him who learns to think only true thoughts about himself and about all in his world. Some wonderful truths have been unfolded to you, and now it surely will be easier for you to do the things you have found you must do, if you would free yourself from the old consciousness and the conditions surrounding you and would enter the new consciousness awaiting.

The way out has been shown you. But - you must walk in it, no one can do that for you.

You cannot be shoved, nor can you jump or slide into the Kingdom - you have to earn your right to enter, have to walk every step of the way there, no matter how difficult and steep grows the path. It is no journey to be taken by the half-hearted and weak-kneed.

If you are now convinced of the truth of what was shown, the next step then is to try to prove its truth, first by getting thoroughly acquainted with this Real Self of you, by seeing Him as yourself, and by going about in His Consciousness. Practice this daily until you actually feel Him within, feel Him giving you of His power, of His vitalizing life and energy, and you thrill at the realization of it.

Then make the determined and unrelenting effort to think only His thoughts and to see and hear only the good and perfection in everything and everyone, resolutely shutting your eyes and mind to appearances and looking right through them to the good they hide.

You can do this - if you will. You can find good anywhere -if you truly look for it.

For with such a desire in your heart you connect up with the good -- your God Consciousness-within, which will illumine your mind and enable you to see with your Spiritual eyes and to hear with your Spiritual ears what is hidden from mortal consciousness.

With every loving desire to please this God-You, you will find help given you to do it, especially when you earnestly put your trust in Him. When you do thus trust Him, you will learn what He means when He says: "If you abide in Me, and let My Words abide in you, you can ask what you will and it will be done unto you." For when your trust becomes absolute you will not want anything any more, for you will know that all He is and has is yours. And there will be no more need to ask, as He will be giving you continually of the riches of His Kingdom, whose store is inexhaustible.

This then, dear friend, is what we would have you do to strive every moment of the day, no matter what you are doing, to abide in His Consciousness, to put all your trust in Him, leaving everything to Him, KNOWING that He will do all things through you perfectly, as you keep your mind free from doubts, feats, worries, untrue thoughts, and concern about results. For you thus enable him truly and freely to live. His life in you, do His will in you, be His Self in you, even as He intended and has been preparing you for all your mortal life.

X. GOD AND MAMMON

In the following verses from the Sermon on the Mount is found all that anyone needs to know who is facing the tribulations now being visited upon humanity and is seeking the reason and purpose of it all and how to be free from them.

We will point out to you how wonderfully it all applies to this very question we have been discussing and how it perfectly confirms all that was stated. We will start with these significant words:

"No man can serve two masters; for either he will hate the one and love the other; or else he will cling to the one and neglect the other. You cannot serve God and mammon."

Think carefully what this means. How many of you are not trying to serve two masters? Yes, you are trying to serve God, but who of you at the present time are not fearing money and its power? Who are not bowing down before it, daily acknowledging its power over you, afraid to do anything because of the control it has over most of your thoughts and acts? In fact is not its influence such that it receives now ten times - nay, one hundred times-more of your thoughts than does God?

And yet you say you are not serving mammon!

Dear friends, you cannot continue this way. You cannot any longer serve two masters. The time has come when you must decide whom you will serve -God or mammon. For why think you these tribulations are being visited upon mankind? It is because in the past you have been trying to serve both God and mammon, and now both have withdrawn their support and are letting you cast for yourself.

So you are finally learning that you of yourself can do nothing, and you are now facing the necessity of choosing whom you will serve and to whom you will give all your allegiance -for when you do choose that is what will be required of you.

And this applies particularly to all seekers after Truth, but includes also those who may in any way have claimed God's help. For those who are truly serving Him, placing all their trust in Him, are unaffected by present conditions and are continually prospered.

While those who have given full allegiance to mammon are likewise greatly prospered seemingly; but their time of reckoning has not yet come.

We are not interested in the latter, however.

Our thoughts are for you -you who are anxious to serve God and to free yourself from the power of mammon forever. To you Jesus' words are especially directed. Hear them, for they are actual promises and contain very definite and unmistakable instructions for you:

"Therefore I say unto you, Be not anxious about your life, what you shall eat, or what you shall drink; nor about your body, what you shall wear. Is not the life of more value than food, and the body than raiment?

"Observe the birds of the air; for they sow not, neither do they reap, nor gather into barns; yet your heavenly Father feeds them. Are you not of greater value than they?

"Besides, which of you by being anxious can prolong his life one moment? And why are you anxious about raiment? Consider the lilies of the field how they grow; they toil not neither do they spin; and yet I tell you, that Solomon in all his glory was not arrayed like one of these.

"Wherefore, if God so clothes the grass of the field, which today is and tomorrow is cast into the oven, shall He not much more clothe you, O ye of little faith?"

Here you are told plainly the difference between what is required of those who would serve God and those who serve mammon. The former are clearly shown that they need not be overly concerned about the affairs of their life -about food, drink and clothes; for they are promised that God will take care of all these things if they trust Him. Besides they know that it is His life that is in them, even as in the birds and the lilies, and surely He will feed and clothe and provide for His own life.

But does mammon require such trust? No, he ever holds over his servants the whip of fear of loss, lack and poverty until they become abject slaves to his slightest wish.

The former in their efforts to please God develop and portray a life of loving and selfless service. While the latter as they yield more and more to mammon develop into cold and heartless beings, thinking only of how to satisfy their utterly selfish lusts. But listen further to Jesus' words:

"Therefore be not anxious saying, what shall we eat or what shall we drink, or wherewithal shall we be clothed?

"For all these the Gentiles seek, and your heavenly Father knows you have need of all these things.

"But seek ye first the kingdom of God and His righteousness; and all these things shall be added unto you."

The Gentiles was a term used by the Jews as synonymous with "heathen" or those who were not of the "chosen people of God," and undoubtedly Jesus used it with that meaning.

In other words, the chosen of God, His servants, know Him and trust him fully for all their needs. But the Gentiles, those who are not His people, are the ones who are always anxious about what they shall eat or drink or how they shall be clothed.

So Jesus tells us that if we will make first the seeking of the Kingdom of God - the Divine Consciousness where love and peace abide, putting all our trust in God and giving all our service to Him -all the things needed in the physical world will be richly provided.

The Emphatic Diaglot translation from the original Greek states they will be "superadded."

"Be not anxious then for the morrow, for the morrow will have its own problems. Sufficient for each day are the problems thereof." How much more plainly can it be declared to us that we are being lovingly watched over and cared for, that all our needs are known and will be supplied, and that our only thought should be a knowing that everything will be provided for us, even as God provides for the birds and the lilies?

Then it all resolves itself in a matter of trusting and abiding, and of doing the thing that is right before us to do the very best we know how, leaving the results, tomorrow and all else to God. Can you bring yourself to do this, dear friends? You must decide now. This is the time when we must choose on which side we will stand. Only a little while remains.

Whom then are you going to serve? Do you require more tribulations and harder tests to help you decide?

But remember it can no longer be a halfhearted or a divided service. That will not be any longer permitted. The hopelessness of such should have been proved to you from former efforts. You must give up all - all that you have and are -and follow Him; must make Him and the finding of His Kingdom and the living of His life FIRST in your consciousness. It must be an every-moment-of-the-day trusting; the thought of Him must supersede every other thought.

That is the kind of trusting He now seeks from you. And oh, the joy and blessedness of those who have given themselves over wholly to Him in such trusting!

THE END

BOOK FOUR
WEALTH

YOU, to whom I have given an abundance of that which the world calls Riches, hearken unto this My special Message to you.

You!

Who are you, that you should be thus blessed above your brothers?

Who are you, that you should be given such a privilege, when millions of your fellows apparently have nothing?

Have you ever asked yourself that question? Have you ever satisfactorily answered it?

Or perhaps you think YOU did it all; that you have no one to thank for these so-called blessings but yourself?

Think you this is so?

Let us see.

Did you ever wonder WHY you were born as you were, into the particular conditions that surrounded your entrance into this life?

Did you ever wonder why you had to contend with the particular conditions that surrounded and confronted you all along your journey up through life?

Did you ever wonder why YOU came equipped with the certain tendencies, qualities and powers of mind and soul you had while your brothers and sisters and even your parents were so entirely different or came much less fortunately equipped?

Have you arrived at any satisfactory conclusion?

No?

Then listen!

I AM responsible for all this. I did it all. I chose those conditions for you to be born into. I created every condition you met in life, and forced you through them, and through every experience of whatsoever nature. It was I who brought you to where you are today.

You, of yourself, did nothing. That personality you call yourself is merely an automation which I move to suit My purpose.

I

Who am I?

I, Who speak with so much assurance and authority?

Be Still and Know.

I Am YOU, Your TRUE Self;

That higher, purer, supernal part of you that arouses itself as you read, which sits back and listens and judges, and points out the truth of these words to your consciousness, and which from the beginning has guided and taught you all the Truth you know today.

Not that personality you show to the world and which you THINK is yourself; not that proud, selfish mask of a self that has been feeding you on error all these years.

For I AM your REAL Self, that Something in you which you KNOW has made you all you REALLY are, that has inspired, and cautioned, and chided, and urged, and led you on and on, despite hardships, obstacles, suffering, failure, until you have, in a dim, half-conscious way grown to rely upon it, without knowing definitely why.

Yes, I AM that Something. I AM that Divine SELF of you, abiding deep within your human personality, almost stifled by its worldly ideas, its selfish desires, its foolish pride and ambitions, yet ever seeking, longing, yearning to make you conscious of My existence, of My REAL Identity.

Yes, My Child, that Something AM I, I, Who from the beginning have been sitting here within, quietly waiting for this moment. Yet while waiting it was really I Who was guiding you all the time, Who put each thought into your mind, made you do everything you did, and Who utilized the foreknown result of each thought and act so as eventually to bring you and others to a final conscious recognition of Me.

And if I have permitted you to feed on these worldly ideas, to follow these selfish desires, to grow fat with pride, and even to gain the summit of all your ambitions, it was only that you might learn the hollowness of it all, and that you could awaken to the realization that there is something else, something which the SOUL of you yearns to bring forth.

Yes, I have "blessed" you by giving you all these things you sometime in the past desired, desired so strongly that you FORCED Me to give them to you. For Desire is the agent of My Will, and supplies you with everything you want, if you want it with sufficient power to compel It to serve you.

But have these things proved the blessings you thought and expected? Have you gotten out of them real enjoyment, and is your heart now at peace?

If not, why?

It is only because you have failed to recognize Me, your True Self, as the Giver, and have used them not at all in My service, but only to satisfy your own selfish pleasure.

But I have allowed you to indulge yourself to your heart's content with all such empty joys, even leading you on from one to another, holding out to you the possibility of finding in some new bauble, or sensation, or accomplishment, or power, that something you craved, but which, alas! you have never found and never even glimpsed, — except, perhaps, when in the hours of deeper remorse and penitence you turned from this world of self you created around you to the Ideal within, and dimly sensed THERE My Presence.

Ah, dear son, I have indeed given you these blessings, and they ARE *REAL* blessings; for they are My special sign of approval to YOU.

But the blessings are not what you think them to be. The real blessings are in the qualities I have developed in you in the acquirement of these riches, in the attainment of these desires, — the qualities of determination to win, of persistency of purpose, the power to do, the ability to master every natural fault and weakness that stand in the way; all of which are but different phases of My Will, the USE of which I have been teaching you, that later on I can manifest in and through you, with your consent, My Will in Spiritual ways, even as you have been manifesting It in worldly ways.

In other words, all attaining, whether it be of money, power or fame — in art, literature or music, science, philosophy or religion, is but so much training in the USE of My Will; and therefore labor, business, science, religion, the arts or the professions, are merely incidents, or the outer means I use to develop in you the CONSCIOUS use of My Will.

You may think it is YOUR will that is so acting, but so long as you consider yourself as separate from Me, and you use this will only to please yourself, it naturally is self-will, and that is why it brings you no lasting or tangible good, only trouble, unhappiness and heartache, when the novelty of possession wears off. And so, of course, you cannot know

Me, and therefore cannot acknowledge that ALL that you do, or have, or suffer, is but the result of the action of MY Will working thus in and through you to bring about My Purpose.

But the time is coming when you will understand somewhat of this. Hence this Message. Hence this special favor to you.

You may ask, why I, God, the Omnipotent One, the all Good, the all Wise, made such an unequal distribution of My Blessings, of My Substance, of My Intelligence, of the use of My Will, giving to the few the vast surplus and to the many such a pitiful lack.

You may well ask, for that is the problem I have given you, and all, to solve.

But as I have enabled you partly to solve this problem, even though you do not know it, I will now disclose to you some of its apparent mysteries.

II

KNOW, My son, that I give no thing to anyone unless that thing has been earned by him. By earned, I mean, grown ready for it, through desiring it so strongly that he finally draws from Me, his all-powerful, perfect SELF within, sufficient life-force and vital energy to compel conditions and circumstances to yield up and other intelligences to supply the necessary means and substance to provide form or actuality for that thing.

So it is that sometime in the past, either in this life or in a previous existence, you had arrived at the point where I could inspire in you the Idea of possessing Wealth.

I could do this, for you had grown in Soul stature and strength so that it had come time to awaken and develop in you certain of your Soul qualities and faculties which I needed for use in My service.

So I implanted in your mind the Idea of possessing Wealth or Riches. This Idea, following the usual course of Nature, in the process of time, put forth its rootlets within the soil of world conditions. These rootlets of determination, persistence, daring, doing, saving, seeing only success ahead, undiscouraged by obstacles, never recognizing failure, pushed their way unerringly to the most fertile soil through and past all obstacles, deep into the earth nature. Likewise and at the same time a little shoot from the Idea pushed its way up towards the light and

113

gradually began to show itself above the surface of your mental and material life. This shoot, which was the STOCK of the Idea of Wealth, grew fast, when once firmly rooted, and it soon became a sturdy, wide-spreading tree.

That tree is the outward manifestation of your life today. The nature and kind of a tree is what your character is. Its leaves are your money; its fruit just what the possession of that money has meant to you. If there is decay or unsoundness in root, trunk or branch, it is because of error, wrong or disease somewhere in the tree, which finally will destroy it unless remedied or removed.

Is there any error, wrong or disease in YOUR tree, My son? Are there any worms gnawing their way into its heart?

Let us see. Let us search deep beneath the surface soil of world conditions, with its finely worked out system of "legitimate" methods, and its politically gained protection of the law. Let us look underneath the bark of selfishness, with its human beliefs and opinions regarding the rights of the strong. Let us peer into the cracks and crotches, the dark places in your life which are carefully hidden from the world. Let us look unflinchingly into all these places, and see if there are not some rotten spots.

Have you attained all this Wealth by absolutely honorable and righteous methods? Has any part of it been gained by sharp business practices, — yes, legitimate from the law's standpoint, but not from Mine, your True Self? Was part of it gained by deception of friends or partners? Part by taking advantage of trusts imposed in you? Part by going through bankruptcy and settling for a percentage of your just debts? Part by riding roughshod over weaker Souls? Part by deliberate fraud? Part by any means which aroused a protesting voice within you, and which voice, in moments of quiet and solitude, ever appears to remind and accuse?

Ah, My dear child, can you truly say that none of the Wealth you possess is thus tainted?

Yes, I know, and understand.

And dear one, if you have suffered, and have regretted, and are now seeking to make restitution, it is because you have listened to My Voice, and are beginning to recognize and long for My guiding influence in your life.

But if you deny, and loudly proclaim that none of the above applies to you, and you still refuse to listen to My loving Voice within, wee, faint, almost drowned by the loud tumult now going on in your heart, — know, dear one, that you, too, must suffer, must enter into a life of heartache and misery and sorrow, into which I must plunge you, in order to purge your Soul of the pride, self-will and self-love that now control you; so that you, too, can awaken to My Love and thus learn to hear and know My Voice, ever seeking to point out to you the true way of Life.

As for your brothers, many, very many, I do not yet deem ready to receive the Idea of acquiring Wealth. In many others the Idea has been planted, and they are merely feeling the quickening power of Desire, My agent. Others are forced by Desire to think and strive, and are beginning to see the means of future acquirement. And still others are in the act of producing tangible results.

With all, however, I AM merely using the Idea of Wealth, and the motive power of Desire for its acquirement, to develop those Soul qualities and mental faculties which will enable Me finally and fully to bring into manifestation their Real Self, I, God within them, that through them My Will may be made manifest on earth even as It is in Heaven.

With you, My blessed one, in whom I have brought to complete fruition My Idea of Wealth in the form of Money and Possessions, and who as My custodian are now capable and ready consciously to co-operate with Me in its use in My Service, when you can be convinced that I, God, will direct you in such use, — know that soon, very soon, you will become conscious that I AM within you, and that you need not go without to any other authority to learn this great fact. For I will cause you to KNOW that I AM leading and guiding you, and will gradually open up to your consciousness My Plan and Purpose for the Use and distribution of ALL that I have given you.

You, who have already heard My Voice within, and are seeking to satisfy Me by giving a portion of your wealth to churches, or libraries, or scientific research, or charity, or settlement work, or other enterprises thinking My Voice can be stilled that way, and that the yearning hunger in your heart may be thus appeased:

Know that such acts are all in vain, for never can I thus be satisfied. My Voice will become only more insistent, as you strive by giving merely a portion of the wealth you hold and which is ALL Mine and none of it yours, in such effort to please Me.

For, My child, I AM already pleased with you. Are you not what I have made you? Is not all you have done what I permitted and even caused you to do?

And if I have permitted you to try to propitiate Me by using your Wealth in such manner, it is only because such was all I could make you understand at the time of My Purpose surging within you.

Therefore, when, in your desire to please Me, you attract to you many who ask you to give of your abundance to this or that charity, to this or that project for helping humanity, and what you call your business judgment tells you what is given will not be used properly or wisely for such purposes, and you do not respond, — know that you have likewise been led thus to refuse by Me, Who thus chose for you, even as I chose for you to give to those other enterprises; and all this for the fulfilling of My Purpose.

For I have not only reserved this Wealth I have given you for a special Service, and I have chosen you as My Agent in its distribution in the way I shall disclose to you all in due season; but I AM preparing your human mind so that you can understand it is not your Wealth I want, but YOU. I want you to know that you and I are One; that I, your REAL Self, must now rule; that self-will and self-pleasure must die, and My Will and My Pleasure must live and be FIRST and ALL with you from now henceforth.

Therefore, I AM preparing your mind so that I can speak direct to your Soul consciousness from within, and I AM quickening your heart so you can become wholly conscious of My Presence therein.

So, beloved, if I say I want YOU, ALL of you; heart, soul, mind, body, — all you are, all you have, all you ever hope to be or have, I say it because I want My own, — YOU the mortal expression of My Self.

The time has come when you must know We are ONE, that there is no separation, no difference — only as you think there is. Hence, all you have or are is Mine and always has been Mine and Mine only. And now I claim My own.

My own MUST come to Me. My claim you MUST recognize. And you MUST give back ALL, – every penny, your home, lands, securities, business; your body, intellect, heart, faculties, will, your whole personality — every loved possession, even the dearest treasure of your heart.

For not until you have brought all and laid them at My feet, and said, *"Here, Father, take ALL. Take and use, and only let me serve Thee. Command and henceforth I will obey;"*

Not until you thus come in true humility, with a desire as strong to give to Me as the one which impelled you to get for self; not until your Soul is so possessed with a yearning to serve Me and to rest Its wearied heart in My Love that It can no longer be denied, — can you ever enter into My Kingdom.

Long ago to another people I said, "It is easier for a camel to go through a needle's eye than for a rich man to enter the kingdom of God."

This is just as true today. For he whom I have deemed worthy to express the qualities of Soul I AM now expressing through you cannot easily humble himself, — cannot reduce that haughty personality, which so long has led and ruled, so he can go through the narrow gate of self-abnegation and self-denial.

Yet I say unto you, you must come to that if you would enter into My Kingdom.

This is all foolishness, you say. You cannot enter the Kingdom of God here on earth. Even if you could, you would have to be shown of what practical value such an attainment was to one in business, with a family and all the associations and responsibilities of large and varied interests.

Let us see if it is not possible to find that Kingdom and to enter it right here on earth.

III

LISTEN! And ponder.

Are you not seeking happiness, peace, health, love, the fullness of life here on earth?

Think you you will find them in the things and practices of the world? Have you not learned the futility of that?

Think you you can be truly rich and truly happy, when millions of your brothers are in poverty and misery?

No, My child; not until you have risen above all the illusions of this world of yours, have had your sight cleared by misery and suffering, have felt the poverty of love, have hungered for the TRUE Bread of Life, and have finally gotten a taste of it through forgetting self and serving your brothers, with My Righteousness as the guiding influence of your life, — can you ever find true happiness, find that peace, that harmony, that love your Soul craves. But when you HAVE found THAT, then you have indeed entered into My Kingdom.

I AM come to you now to help you find that Kingdom, to make you aware of My Presence, I, that Something deep down in your heart that yearns for the highest, for PERFECT expression; that craves for the true riches of life, which now you know all the money in the world cannot supply.

I, God, within you, AM speaking straight from out the depths of your heart, from My Kingdom there, sweeping aside all your accumulation of worldly ideas, beliefs and opinions, and am talking direct to your Soul consciousness.

For the time is come when you must awake to your Divine mission, to the REAL purpose of your coming into this world, into this life, into this personality, into the possession of these qualities, this ability, which entitled you to be the custodian of the Wealth I have given you, — but only for such purpose.

The time is come for you to know this, to know Me, that within you which gave you this desire for wealth, which gave you the power to acquire it, which inspired and impelled and guided your every effort to attain it, and finally which now gives you the desire to use SOME of it in My Service.

Can you not see that Something is I, your own True Self, yes, God within you, the only God you will ever know, the God Who is not only dwelling and working thus in the Kingdom within you, but within your every brother, be he high or low, rich or poor, wise or ignorant; the God Who is gradually evolving your human personalities, with their mortal bodies, minds and intellects, so that He can eventually through you express ALL of His Divine qualities, even as it is in Heaven?

So I have been evolving and unfolding you so that I can find perfect expression through you, just as I evolve the Rose, first the bud-shoot, then the bud, finally unfolding its petals, — so that through it I can show forth some of My perfect fragrance and beauty.

But you I have chosen to be a CONSCIOUS worker and expressor with Me. I have chosen you to be the means by which I AM going to bring great Joy and Happiness into this world of sorrow, discouragement, discontent and misery. I have chosen you to be the avenue through which I AM going to pour many Blessings into the hearts and lives of thousands of your brothers.

Would you like to work thus with Me. My son?

Would you not like to be such an avenue to participate in this Joy and Happiness, to become a partner with Me in its distribution, — with Me, your own True Self?

Think! Think what it would mean!

Is it possible? Could you really be a participator? you ask.

Yes, and all you need to do is to turn within to Me, with perfect Faith and Trust, and let Me show you the way. All it needs is for you to be CONSCIOUS of Me, abiding thus in your heart, inspiring your every thought word and act, no longer listening to self-will and self-interest, but only to Me, your Higher Self, as I tell you of My plans and open up to you the wonderful visions of what I have in store for you, if you faithfully follow My instructions.

Ah, My son, if you only would! If you only could know the Glory that awaits compliance with this longing surging in your heart!

Then indeed would you be in Heaven, right here on earth. And such Joy and Peace and Rest would be yours, that your very Soul, even now at the thought of it, almost bursts its bounds in its yearning that it may be.

Then would Life be a continual song of gladness, for the Sun of My Love would shine continuously from out your heart, lighting and blessing you all along the way.

Then would We joyfully start out each day to Our business or task, be it whatever it may, you letting Me do the leading, and you waiting upon My every Word, resting and trusting absolutely in My Wisdom and Judgment, KNOWING that the thing We do will always be just the RIGHT thing, and that all that We do will bring SUCCESS, no matter what We undertake.

How would you like to form such a partnership, My son?

Would that not be better than spending most of your time worrying about business or investments, or what to do with surplus, income, or profits, in order to get the most returns for them; fearing continually, when approached by friends or acquaintances, that they are trying to interest you in some favorite scheme, or in some unwise speculation, or some craftily conceived plan to relieve you of some of your money?

Yes, if you would but enter into partnership with Me, letting Me be the elder partner throwing all responsibility upon Me, then indeed would you be relieved of all this; and you would find, instead of cares and burdens and problems, now so exacting they leave you not one moment's peace of mind, that all this has been lifted from you forever, and Life has become one glad round of happy days, filled to the brim with Soul-satisfying experiences, because wholly devoted to making others happy.

IV

And now, My son, what say you?

What are you going to do about it?

I have shown you who and what you are; that you are nothing; that I AM, and you are NOT, — you being only one of My mortal expressions, which I have brought into being in order to manifest on earth through you some of My Divine qualities, and to bring Joy and Peace and Good-Will into the hearts of many of My other and less complete expressions.

I have shown you all this. And you may not believe it. But that makes no difference. You can believe or not, as you choose. But whichever you choose, know it is really I Who choose, and not you. And if you disbelieve, it is only because I AM not yet ready for you to entertain this belief; for you still have many disillusionments, disappointments, heartaches and sufferings to go through before you can come into true understanding of My meaning.

But mark you, My son! The words I herein speak are seeds I AM planting in your heart and they will germinate, and the time will come when the Truth of them will appear plainly to your understanding.

Then you will know I AM in you, that I AM YOU, that I, your TRUE Self, must and will rule; and that all I have said herein shall blossom forth in actual manifestation in your life.

You who understand and whose heart urges you to enter into full partnership with Me; you, beloved, I here promise, shall soon partake of the Heavenly Joy that awaits.

In the meantime, your work lies before you. You must BE STILL, and learn to KNOW I AM GOD, WITHIN you. You must study and meditate on this and My other Revelations. You must realize that I, God, AM all that there is; that I gave you all, and that I can take away all.

You must accustom yourself to this Truth, and must make ready to give back all to Me for USE in My service.

But, dear son, in giving all to Me, fear not; I, God, AM no outside person, I AM only your Real Self, your own True, Wonderful Perfect SELF.

I ask you to give to no one but Me, your TRUE Self, and then only that I may direct and guide you in its USE. Instead of holding for self, you now will hold for Me. Instead of seeking your pleasure, you now will seek only Mine.

Henceforth you are to abide in Me and let My Words abide in you, and just to the extent you do this, you can ask what you will and it will be done unto you.

BE Still! — and KNOW — I AM — God.

Know that I AM holding in reserve for you wonderful uses for the Wealth I have brought into manifestation through you, uses different from any I have heretofore shown unto man. I have long been preparing you so that you can cooperate with Me in such use.

How would you like to see Man, your brothers, many of them, thousands of them, hundreds of thousands, quickened as you have been quickened with the realization of My Presence within? How would you like to see them awakened to the consciousness of the possession of qualities and powers similar to those you possess, and which, with Me to guide and direct their use, will lift them and you to such heights your human minds now cannot conceive?

How would you like to see the down-and-outs, the failures, the discouraged, the discontented, the weak, the sick, all awakened to their Divine heritage, to the knowledge that ALL that I, the FATHER, have is theirs; and that each and all can be shown HOW to attain it — all that WANT to know, and ASK to be shown?

How would you like to live in a community, in a world, where all were alike expressing My highest qualities and powers, where each was seeking so to eliminate his personality, with all its limited selfish ideas, beliefs and opinions, that My Perfect Life can express?

Would that not be a beautiful world? Would that not be the real Heaven?

Dear son, that is what is coming into manifestation. It is coming despite all appearances to the contrary. The realization of this Heaven has already come to many. It is coming soon to many more, and later to all, as My quickening Power is brought to them, even as It has now been brought to you, and which first must come from without before it can manifest within.

If you would like to hasten its coming, dear son, I hereby give you that privilege. If you would like to help make it possible that thousands and thousands of your brothers can come into the Great Awakening, can come into possession of My DIVINE Qualities and Powers, then Beloved:

Turn within to Me, and seek earnestly to KNOW My Purpose, Pray unceasingly, until I disclose it all, My Blessed One.

Ask and ye SHALL receive. Seek and ye SHALL find. Knock and it SHALL be opened unto you.

THE END.

BOOK FIVE
THE TEACHER

I

You, who have heard the Call of The Christ, and have consecrated yourself and your life to the service of Humanity;

You who have felt the Divine urge to give to others of the Spiritual blessings you have received;

You, who have assumed the position of Teacher and leader to hungering Souls that have come to you to be fed;--

Hear this, My special Message, to you.

You, beloved, are my chosen Minster. You I have selected to be an avenue through which I shall pour many blessing into the world.

Yes, I have called you apart, and have pointed out to you the vast work there is to do, the millions of sleeping Souls waiting for the touch that will rouse them to a consciousness of the real purpose of their being here, in this life.

I have shown you wherein you can help in this Work, and have proven to you that you are truly helping, by the appreciation and gratitude of those whom I have brought to you and enabled you to help.

Yes, you feel you are not working in vain, and although the way may appear dark and uncertain and the means and ability to continue may not be in evidence, yet something within compels you to keep on, telling you that all will be taken care of in due season-if you prove faithful to the cause you have made your own.

I recall all this to you, even though it may not have appeared thus clearly before to your mortal consciousness. I point this out in order to prepare you for what I now have to say.

for i now desire you to know that I have a definite Plan and Purpose in all this, and that the time is here when you may become conscious coworker with ME in its fulfillment; the point in your Spiritual Life has been reached when your true place in MY Plan and an understanding of My Purpose will be revealed to you--if these words meet with a real response in your heart, and you strive earnestly henceforth to obey the instructions I herein shall give.

I!

Who am I?

I, who speak with so much authority, and make such all-inclusive claims?

Who am I that I can instruct you, and can promise rewards which only God can give?

Listen!

I, AM YOU

Your own True SELF!

I, AM, YOUR True Self, the Spirit of the Christ, Whose call you heard;

I, AM your Higher Self, the quickener,

Whose urge you felt;

I, AM, your Divine self, the giver of all the Blessings you received,-

I AM, GOD, within you.

No, not a separate Spirit, dwelling somewhere within your body.

I AM YOU, Your very SELF!

Yes, I, GOD, AM, YOU, your REAL SELF, all of you, mind, soul, consciousness, will.

I, God, your Real Self, speak herein these words of living Truth.

And the way you may know it is I, Who speak-

If these words find any response within you, then it is because I, your Real Self, thus respond, and compel your attention, that you may seek to understand all of my meaning hidden herein.

But if there is no response within, and your human intellect tells you this is but another attempt to enlist your interest in some other teacher's ideas, and that you have a philosophy of your own and need no instructions from others -It is well.

But know it is not you who thus choose, but I, your all-wise and all-loving Self, Who choose for you. For I have other ideas for you, and will bring you to an understanding of my purpose and of your part in MY Plan, all in due season, when I have fully prepared your human mind and your Soul consciousness so you can receive it.

However, if you hear a Voice within, faint, scarcely intelligible, telling you to read on, and perhaps there may be something of value herein; even though you think you already know your part in MY Plan and are now fulfilling My Purpose,-do not refuse. For it is MY Voice trying to be heard above the tumult in your human consciousness, gently urging you to keep your mind open, to listen carefully for Words of Truth, which I here promise you will appear abundantly, beyond measure, if you truly seek to know the Word of God.

But, in order to get the full meaning of what follows, try to imagine that the "I" speaking herein is your Real self, you Higher Self; and, even if you do not believe it as yet, assume for the time being that it is your Higher Self, and thus endeavor to attain the consciousness of it being YOU, talking to your mortal mind, as if to a separate personality.

If you will persist in holding this consciousness while you read, much, very much will be added unto you in the way of Spiritual blessings, land you will sing glad praises to God that this Message came into your life.

II

You, My beloved child, who are seeking Me, but who have not yet found Me, excepting as an intangible something. Which has uplifted and inspired and led you on and on, ever into narrower and yet brighter paths, compelling you to reach out a helping hand to every needy one you meet:

You, who are conscious of Me as the Christ Love within your heart, and who seek to spread the Message of His Love abroad, sowing it in every heart that appears ready to receive it:

You, to whom I have come to radiant flashes of light, or in visions, either sleeping or waking, as Truth, illumining your mind so that for the time being you see clearly the Reality of My Spiritual Life and the illusoriness of all things that appeal to the outer senses; and you are now seeking to teach others this Truth;

You, who have become conscious of Me as the indwelling Life within you, and it manifests to you as Power, and enables you not only to show forth MY LIFE in your body as vibrant Health, but it permits you to transmit this Life to others, vitalizing, strengthening and healing them, and thus bringing them to the consciousness of MY LIFE within their bodies:

You, whom I have led a little further, whom I have taught the use of some of the laws of MY Being, having quickened in you certain inner faculties and powers, which seemingly set you apart from your fellows, so that you now call yourself an occultist, and are seeking to attain the complete mastery of these powers of self;

Yes, and even you, My Blessed One, who are conscious of Me as your Divine self, as God within you, and who are drawing from Me freely MY LOVE. My Wisdom, and MY Power, and who are teaching this Great Truth and attracting to you many followers who hail you as an Illuminated one:-

To you, one and all, I bring this. My Message of the Impersonal Life.

The idea of the "Impersonal " may not be new to you. You may have pondered over it. You may have striven more or less to live it. You may even have taught it to your followers, and yet you may have no comprehension of its real meaning.

It is My Purpose now to make you conscious of that meaning, so that you as Teacher and Leader to others no more can have the excuse of not knowing it, when I hereafter, from within, insist that MY Impersonal Life shall manifest in and through you. For I, your True self, henceforth will be satisfied with nothing less.

So follow carefully all I now shall say, and seek earnestly to know My real meaning, -its personal and vital application to you,- before passing it by or discarding it, should that impulse come to you.

I AM first going to ask some questions.

In asking these questions, I AM directing them straight to your Soul consciousness. Necessarily they will have to go through your mortal mind. As your mortal mind is but a part of your mortal self or your human personality, it first becomes necessary that you learn the ways of the mortal mind and see this self as it really is--not as you fancy it is,-- see this personality of yours pretends to feel hurt, commence to rebel and deny, and even to grow indignant, if not angry, at these questions. For I AM going to probe to the quick, right to the center of its self-complacency, its self-righteousness, its spiritual pride, its love of power, of leadership, of being thought very wise and good,--if any of these qualities still exist in your personality.......

But remember, it is not you who are feeling hurt, or who rebel or grow angry. It is only your personality. For you are really I, your own True Self, and I AM asking these questions, and I AM showing up to you these qualities, insisting that all that stands in the way of MY Perfect Impersonal Life expression henceforth can have no place in your life.

If you watch carefully and study the thoughts and feelings that come to your mind as you read the questions, you will, perhaps , discover a phase of your nature you thought was no longer in evidence. But the special mission of this Message is to make you fully aware of such phase, and of all phases of your human nature, that have not yet come under MY, your True Self's dominion.

This is inner teaching, and it is an inner work which you will now be called upon to do, with ME, your own Higher Self, as Teacher.

If your Soul responds, and you fearlessly are willing to accept anything I have to say, and will accept it in true humility and understanding of Spirit, know that great Spiritual Joy awaits you and many Blessings will follow.

But if your personality still insists that the "I" speaking herein is merely some person, who considers him or herself divinely ordained, and who is taking an unwarranted liberty in thus obtruding into your private affairs; and that you need not answer the questions even to yourself, for they are no one's business but your own; if your personality, with its merely human mind, so persuades you,--it is well, and I needs must teach you in some other and much harder way.

Yet it is all true; these questions are no one else's business. They are only your business. But remember, I, your own True self, God within you, alone AM asking them. And I. Am ASKING THEM ONLY THAT YOU MAY FACE YOUR SELF, that you may see clearly this personality of yours, with all its human weaknesses, faults and misconceptions that still exist, and which, through your inability to perceive their subtle influence over you, are hindering the perfect expression of My Impersonal Life in and through you.

And if I shall prick the bubbles of all such illusions of the personality still lurking around in your mental atmosphere, after first showing up clearly their unreality, it is only in order that, should they again appear, you will immediately recognize them and refuse them entrance into your life.

Perhaps your personality is saying, as you read, that none of this applies to you, that you need no such instructions.

Think you so? Then answer to Me, your True Self, the following questions, carefully studying your feelings, after reading each, with soul-searching analysis;--

Are you sure. My child, there is nothing of self, seeking for self, in this work you claim to be doing for Humanity?

Are you sure you, personally, are not taking the credit for the help your students and followers are getting through you?

Are you quite sure you are not feeling a secret pleasure and pride in their attitude of admiring respect and awe towards you?

These teachings you are giving out,--are you certain they are direct from Me, your Divine self? Or are they but your personal views, the thoughts you have gathered from other human teachers?

Are you tainting this Work, I have given you to do by subtly introducing your personality into it, drawing attention more to you as a teacher, than turning them to Me within themselves, their only true Teacher?

Can you truly say you have only loving and helpful thoughts, and speak only The Christ's words, when asked or when talking about other teachers and leaders, no matter who they be?

When meeting with other teachers and leaders, do you never push your self forward, never desire to lead or impress them with your personality or your powers?

When you meet one who has come into a higher realization of God than you, does only the purest, brotherly love go out from you to that Soul?

When one of your own pupils, through your aid, awakens to the presence of ME within, and quickly attains to an even greater consciousness of My Powers than have you, do you sincerely rejoice with great rejoicing, and praise God for His Blessings to that one?

Are you sure, beloved, you are doing all that you do without thought of reward, caring naught for results, resting only in the consciousness that I AM doing it all, and that i AM responsible?

Do you truly realize that you and your personality are one, that there is no difference: and do you fully understand your

Own self, and know your identity with ME, God, your Divine Self?

In all your teachings of these high Truths, do you, in your Soul, recognize the Oneness of ALL; that I, God, am All there is: that ALL there is you are: that I AM your Real Self;

that there is no separation: that all that you do God does: that you are One with God, and all God's powers are your powers?

Are you sure, My child, that all the things you are teaching you, yourself, ARE: that you are doing, manifesting, LIVING all that you preach to others?

If you can truly answer satisfactorily to ME, your Higher Self, all these questions, then this Message is not for you, and you need read no further; for you know already all that I AM going to say.

But if you are not sure, and realize that your personality is still a more or less dominating factor in your life, then it would be wise to read on. For I AM now coming to the vital part of MY Message.

III

Ah, My beloved, how shall I tell you? How can I penetrate through the wall of unconscious self-righteousness, of self-sufficiency, of spiritual pride and independence, which your personality has built up around you, perhaps, and which often prevents My Words of Truth, spoken through others, reaching your Soul consciousness?

How can I get past the feeling which even now, maybe, is flooding your human consciousness, rousing your ire and opposition, so that you may not grasp the deep significance of my meaning?

Can you not see, if such feeling is manifesting in your heart, that your personality is still much in evidence--when it can so control you? Can you not understand that, not until words such as the above, coming from any source whatsoever, can create in you nothing but a sympathetic comprehension of their loving and helpful intent: and that, should any feelings of a rebellious or antagonistic nature arise, not until you can immediately recognize them and their source, and can proceed to transmute them into love and gratitude to Me for thus pointing out to you these weaknesses that still exist--can you be a pure and true channel through which the Christ teachings can flow?

Can you not see that when one sets one's self up as a teacher to others, and assumes to act as a mediator between them and God, and to interpret for them His Will and His Meaning, that one takes upon one's self a great responsibility,--unless one is resting wholly in the consciousness of God and His Love, so that God is able to speak and act through one's human mind and body without let or hindrance of any kind?

And it is to enable the sincere and true seeker after God, him who would earnestly strive to abide in Him and to let His consciousness abide in his heart, if he but knew how: him who years only to know His Will, that he may obey it and serve Him in every possible way, --it is to enable such to know I, the True Self within, AM God, beyond peradventure of a doubt, that these words are written.

There are many professing to know Me, to be followers of Me, to be giving out My teachings, and who are teaching and preaching the way of atonement; but, who outwardly to others, and in their innermost thoughts, are so mixed up with their personalities, are so influenced and controlled by them, that they do not know Me, even though they proclaim daily that I am leading them and speaking through them. It is for such also, that these Words are intended.

It is true I do speak through such: but not as they understand. For they, personally, even through priding themselves over the beautiful thoughts that flow from their mouths at times, and the help these thoughts are to others, know not when I speak and when their personality. For if they did truly know Me, they would have no pride, would take no credit to or thought of themselves; but would humbly abide in the consciousness of Me doing it all, and would let Me and My Impersonal Love rule in every detail of their lives.

Yet I speak through such proud personalities, and even through hypocrites and teachers of false doctrines, using every avenue to bring to the seeking Soul the phases of Truth needed to lead it into conscious oneness with Me. For remember, truth is not always sugarcoated, and ofttimes it is needful that one taste of the bitter in order to appreciate the sweet and the pure.

Know you not it is through your sins, your mistakes, through deception, false friends, wrong teaching, that you learn and grow strong? Thus principally do I teach.

I lead you through all these, that you may learn to distinguish the truth from the false, the realities of life from the fallacies and illusions. The suffering and pain such learning entrails is only the fire of My Love in your heart burning away the lusts of the flesh, the error thoughts, the selfishness, pride and egotism, implanted and fostered therein by the personality, which must be removed that My Impersonal Life can freely and fully manifest.

And this personality, what is it? It is that which you, with your human mind, imagine yourself to be. It is the creature to which you gave birth many, many ages ago, which you have nurtured and fed, loved and fought for, trusted and followed and believed in, just as if it were real, all these years: the child of your bosom, the creature of your human mind, thought-born, when you fell away in consciousness from Me in Eden after your first sin, and even since have fed with and bred on the idea that you were separate from ME, and that I, God, was displeased with you and have been continually punishing you for eating the fruit of the knowledge of Good and Evil.

And if I have permitted you to love and trust, follow and obey this imaginary child, now grown in your consciousness to full maturity, and become so strong and powerful that it dominates and rules its parent with a rod of iron, it is only in order that, through the sins and errors into which it drove you and the consequent suffering these brought, I might awaken you to the reality of its unreality, to the fact that it has no existence except in your mind; that the only life it has and all its power, come from your constant thinking that you are this personality and are separate and apart from Me.

And if there has awakened in you a dim sense of its unreality, and you are now turning within to Me, seeking to be released from the thralldom of its rule, know that it can never be until you are fully conscious that you and I, God within you, are one; that there is no separation: that all I, AM, Are: that all I have is yours: that all power is given you in heaven and earth: and hence that I, AM, you must be Master, and that this personality of your is merely a phase of mortal thought. I permitted to be born in your human consciousness, in order to develop your mind and body until they become strong enough consciously to contain and fully express My Impersonal Life.

You must be Master, absolute Master of yourself. But you cannot be Master until you know yourself, know every phase of your personality;

all your strength and all your weakness: all your powers, physical, mental and spiritual: all your human faults, tendencies and limitations: and can see yourself and know your personality even as others see and know you, with both the eyes and judgment of the world and the vision and understanding of the Spirit: know all about that personality which has so subtly and craftily impinged itself upon your consciousness, that now you can scarcely tell when it is manifesting, and when I, your True self.

So this personality of yours must be subdued, must be merged into MY Impersonality, before MY true Teachings can come forth. You must realize with Soul realization that you, the Impersonal you, the True you, are one with your brother, even as you are one with Me, you must learn to see Me, his Impersonal self, underneath the illusions of his personality, must permit no reflection of your own personality to cloud the clear sight of Me therein, yearningly waiting for the time when he, too, perhaps through you, may be led to recognize Me abiding within his heart.

In the Impersonal all is one. When you can enter into the oneness of the Impersonal consciousness and can abide there at will, you have entered into My Kingdom and have found God: and thereafter will be able to see and know Him in all His creations. For the Impersonal Consciousness is My Consciousness: It is My Kingdom, the realm of my Being: and I, AM, Life of all things, once having entered this realm you become one with Me, and therefore one with all beings, and you can go in and out and find pasture. For I will feed you with the Bread of the Spirit, and the

Wine of Life will flow through you in rivers of Living love, blessing you in all ways and likewise all whom you contact.

IV

So I tell you these things, My child, My chosen one, that you may strive unceasingly to know this personality, know all its subtly selfish phases, many of them hidden so deep within your consciousness that you are not even aware they are there. Because you hid them there long ages ago, having been deceived into believing them good and necessary to your life: and therefore made them part of your nature. But now, with

My help, you are going to hunt them all out and cast them forth, that MY Impersonal Nature can freely manifest.

As I have chosen you, My child, and have called you aside, and have permitted you to think you have a special work to do, I want you to be absolutely sure, beloved, it is My Voice you have been listening to while doing this work, and not the voice of your personality. If I AM to be your Teacher, and you wish Me to lead and direct you in this work, and you truly desire to serve Me, then must every attribute of your human personality yield itself to Me, and you must compel it so to do. So long as one selfish desire or instinct remains, it is sure to taint your work, and you still be under the domination of the personality.

There are many, many ways it will seek to manifest; but I, AM, and I will point out each clearly:--if you ask Me. I will tell you, not with dominating, insistent authority, nor with anxious clamoring within, but with gentle, loving suggestions, that you cannot fail to understand,--if you will but be on the alert and will listen for my Voice, which is ever counseling and directing these who wait upon Me in living faith and trust.

My work; you will gradually learn, can only be done with the spirit of Impersonal love in your heart. Only through such spirit-selfless, disinterested, never caring about results-can I express through you. You must leave all consequences to Me.

When you have learned to do that, then will I cause to quicken in you a consciousness of your identity with Me, of My Power and my Wisdom and My Love within. Then will your personal life gradually merge into MY Impersonal Life, and you will be conscious of all your Divine Heritage and of the real Work I have chosen for you to do.

But until your human consciousness has become merged with My Divine Consciousness, until you can truly know and use your Divine Powers, it might be better to so live that you assume to possess no powers or wisdom above you fellows. It might be better first to prove to yourself that you are able to live and to be all these things you now more or less clearly see with the inner eye, before you give out to others as Truth or as coming from God.

For you know it is only the personality that sets itself up as one of authority, or as being who in the Spirit, as one chosen of God, and as being His mouthpiece. And remember, I, AM, your students and followers, even as i AM in you. Often, very often the beautiful thoughts that come from teachers do not carry the conviction of Truth, because i cause their hearers to see only too plainly that such treaters are not living what they teach; or that their personalities are too dominating; or they are too desirous of giving the impression of possessing wisdom, or spirituality, or powers; or that they are unmistakably leading followers on only in order to get from them what money they can, deceiving themselves the while into believing such fallacious reasoning as "The servant is worthy of his hire," or that "in giving out spiritual teachings one must receive back material pay, "that being the law."

Ah, My beloved, are you sure some of these things are noticed by your pupils or hearers in you? Are you sure that the money question is not occupying the most prominent place in you mind, and the desire to serve Me is receiving but secondary consideration? Can you truly say that you put all material problems wholly up to Me, knowing that I will always provide bounteously: that there is no fear in your heart, no doubts or questions as to My always supplying every need, yes every desire?

If so, then Is it necessary to charge or accept pay for the loving help I give out through you? Is not My servant worthy of his hire, and will I not provide? Consider the lilies of the field and the fowl of the air. Who clothes and feeds them? Are you not more to Me than they? Oh, you of little Faith!

Listen! Only as you give out of the fulness of love, freely, unthinking as to reward or returns, can you receive of My Bounty.

But you may not accept this now. If so, it is well For I have chosen that it be so, and that you learn the Truth through other channels. You must still hold to the belief that even God's servants must live, and that in living and working on the world plane they are compelled to use the world's methods, even in Spiritual work.

And this is true, but not as you understand it. The time will come, however, when you have learned through trial and suffering to know My Way, when you are able to see with My Impersonal eyes and to know with My Impersonal understanding, and can put aside altogether all personal interest in your teaching, and in both the results of and the reward for such teachings--that you will know how to use the world's tools even in Spiritual work.

But before that can be I may have to lead you by the hard way up the high mountain of Spiritual attainment, by the hand way of bitter experience.

Yes, you can get there that way, But, oh, how long and heartbreaking the journey!

Perhaps, you say, that is the only way one can learn.

No, it is only one way you can learn-the hard way. It is the personal way, and it may be necessary for some to go that way. But I seek to save you from that way.

Have you not seen the sad misfortune of some of those I have thus led up into the high mountain, those who have climbed up the hard way,--and have fallen, even from near the summit?

Yes, no one can rise so high but what he can fall; for the personality is always in evidence on that journey. It is the adversary who is opposing every step. That is what makes it so hard. So long as there is left anything of self, just so long will the personality find a way to oppose. I may lead you to the mountain top, and show you all the kingdoms of the air, of the earth, of fire and of water, and present them to you and tell you they are all yours to use. But if you have not thoroughly purged your heart, mind and Soul of self, behold! the personality appears and speaks from behind you, and so subtly imitates MY Voice that you may think it is I. And when it tells you to take and use these kingdoms to glorify, that having climbed to this great height, such is your reward--you may trust it, and obey; yes, even as they who fell from their former high estate, into deep, outer darkness.

In order that you may be saved that journey and that temptation, My beloved. I here hold out to you the far easier and simpler way.

If you will but abide in the consciousness of Me, the True self within you, and let My Holy Impersonal Love abide in you, and will permit it to flow forth freely, unhindered, unconditioned, from your heart to bless all whom you meet, if you will but do this, you may ask of Me whatever you will, and it shall be done for you.

For do you not see, beloved, if you can fully harmonize your life with my Life, by eliminating all phases of the selfish personality, if you will but get out of the way with your personal ideas, beliefs and opinions, so that My Life, which is but My LIVING Love, can freely and fully express forth through you, --that the void left after the personal life is gone will be immediately filled-even as air rushes into a vacuum--with My

Impersonal Life? For My Impersonal life is the real substance of all things, and is ever seeking to express outwardly Its true nature: and all of It that is necessary to fill out and complete My Divine Nature in you will surely flow both into you and through you,-whenever you let it; and will harmonize and bless you and bring into outer tangible manifestations all good things needed to completely round out your human nature, and make for Joy, Happiness, Satisfaction, and peace within your Soul.

V

And shall I now tell you about MY Impersonal Life, how you may consciously live it with Me, and be wholly One with ME, Your True self, Your Father-in Heaven?

Then listen! And meditate long and earnestly on all I now shall say. Do not pass by a single sentence or any one thought in it until My meaning becomes clear.

I seek nothing but to BE and EXPRESS My Self in and through you. My Self is purely Impersonal, for it is the Real Self of every human being. I AM the pure, perfect, selfless, inner nature of every human self, ensouled in their physical bodies, in order to develop them into mediums for the expression of my Divine attributes on earth, even as it is in Heaven. Therefore, you, too, must seek nothing but to be and express your True Self, which is I, you Divine, Impersonal Self. Thereby do you unite your purpose with Mine, your will with My Will, your nature with My Nature, and thus become One with Me, and We become Two-in-One, the Divine estate on earth.

In order that this may Be, we must purge first your heart, then your mind, and then your body, of every sense and inclinations of the personal self. That can only be accomplished by My Holy Impersonal Love, with which I will fill your heart, so that there will be no room in it for any part of self. With the heart purified and sweetened, the mind will attract and think only pure and sweet thoughts, My thoughts, which are always pure Wisdom. Therefore you will see only Purity and Goodness in all things Naturally, then being no more controlled or influenced by wrong thoughts your body will become subservant to My Life, whose vitalizing, purifying and perfecting power will drive from it all inharmonious. Then, with only My Love in your heart, My thoughts in your mind, and my Life in your body, you will know I AM, your own True Self.--for then there will be no other self

Then I AM, your True Self, will go forth in the world, but not be of it. You will no longer be attracted to or by it. But you will see with My eyes, hear with My ears, and know with My understanding all things,. You no longer will see only the outward appearance of things, but you will see them in their Reality. Nothing past, present or future, will be hidden from you; for the limitations of the human nature are no longer there, and in the Spirit there is no time, space, personalities or separation,--All is one.

And you will go forth with the consciousness of this great Impersonal Love within you as the very substance of your nature, and through It I will uplift, strengthen, help and bless all whom I will lead you to or attract to you. Love being your nature and on the earth plane in man It being the pure and perfect expression of MY Life. It is always full, complete, harmonious outer manifestation.

And with the consciousness of your Divinity and of the Divine Power My Love gives you, instead of parading such or giving evidence of such in my personal way, you will only give and help and bless Impersonally, seeking to remove all fetters, all hindrances, all limitations that prevent My Life in any way from expressing in and through your fellow beings.

Thus you become one with the One Life, with My Inner, Impersonal Life; therefore One with Me, the Fount and Source of all blessings, earthly and Divine. And therefore you will no longer seek to teach or lead others, because you have become Impersonal and being Impersonal you will let Me, within both them and you, do all the teaching and directing. You will no longer seek to lead, but only to follow ME.

And you will no longer seek to be wise, or good, or strong, or rich, or healthy, or happy, because you are all these things, being One with Me, Who AM the inner essence of which these things are but the outer manifestations.

And you will know that all inharmony presages the coming harmony: that all lack is but My urge towards complete expiation; and that all darkness is but shadow indicating the direction of the Light; that all weakness is part of the effects of training which will result in a perfected will; and that all evil is good and necessary, to one who has attained to My Impersonal consciousness and viewpoint.

And so you will go about your business, whatever it be, for then you will know that all business is My business; and instead of seeking and striving to gain for self the Spiritual blessings that lie at the mountain top, you will cease all seeking and striving, and will have forgotten self; and will feel only the urge to give, and give, and give, of the Great Love within, letting It quicken and awaken and help and strengthen the struggling souls about you, seeing to comprehend and obey the feeling of Me within their hearts, but who, owing to their immature and untrained minds, are misunderstanding that feeling and consequently My meaning, as I try to make it known from within.

And I will lead them to you or you to them, that I may teach them first from without through you. Just as I have brought to you My Message through these words, so will I give My Message to many hundreds of others through words I shall speak through you. But his cannot be as I purpose it, until I can live My Impersonal Life in you, until you have yielded up your human personality to My Divine Impersonality. Not until you determine with all the power of your will, and yearn with all the hunger of your Soul, to Live the Impersonal Life, to make your personal self wait upon and serve Me, your own, True, Impersonal Self, can I give you even a glimpse of my Real Meaning.

But when I have vouchsafed you that glimpse, My beloved, ever afterward will the glory of it be with you, and it will lead you on and on, and every on, until My full meaning is forced from Me by the Might of your Soul's Desire.

That is My Message. Its mission is to awaken in you this Desire, the desire to live the Impersonal Life.

This is high teaching, and is only for those who can see it, for those whom I have prepared and made ready for its reception.

To such, however, it is but the door, which opens to far higher teachings, that I will give to them direct from out their own Souls.--those who come to Me in loving faith and trust, and who are willing to empty their hearts of self, that I may fill them with MY Holy Impersonal Love.

For I here promise you,--I have in store for those who yearn to come to Me by the simple, loving, Impersonal way, great wonders of Spiritual Blessings, which will be to them a source of endless Joy; and that I will give to them as I abide in them and they in Me, the unlimited use of ALL of My Divine Powers and Attributes........

The End.

Manufactured by Amazon.ca
Bolton, ON